AMY ~~BRADLEY~~
KATHERINE SEMLER

RUNNING
ON
EMPTY

NAVIGATING THE DANGERS OF
BURNOUT AT WORK

ADVANCE PRAISE

"An important and timely book. Amy and Katherine use compelling personal stories to show how experiences of burnout are shaped by organizational structures and values. Values that put too much work at the centre of our lives. Their insightful analysis suggests practical ways for managers and workers to discuss how their organization can become 'listening systems,' and design work rooted in agency and worthwhile contribution with the ultimate aim of rebalancing work in meaningful and dignified lives. Essential reading."

DR RUTH YEOMAN
Fellow, Kellogg College, University of Oxford

"Burnout is exhaustion, cynicism and losing any sense of personal achievement and agency. It's a terrifying place to find yourself – especially as it is brought on by doing the very things you should enjoy. This excellent and timely study breaks down what is going on. Through research and stories, it builds knowledge in a way that will help many. A triumph of a book."

KERRI-ANN O'NEILL
People and Transformation Director, Ofcom

"One of the toughest leadership challenges is knowing how to get the best out of ourselves and others without going too far. The stories in this book bring to life various versions of 'too far' in a way that is emotionally impactful and practically useful. Today's leaders will benefit greatly from reading them."

BARNEY QUINN
Former CEO, Telefónica HISPAM Sur and
Former Global CHRO, Telefónica Group

"Through the lived experience of others, we can better protect ourselves and those we lead. This book brings a unique lens on burnout through its storied approach and is a must-read for contemporary leaders."

PROFESSOR STEVEN HAMS MBE
Chief Nursing Officer

Published by
LID Publishing
An imprint of LID Business Media Ltd.
LABS House, 15-19 Bloomsbury Way,
London, WC1A 2TH, UK

info@lidpublishing.com
www.lidpublishing.com

A member of:

businesspublishersroundtable.com

Printed by Severn, Gloucester
ISBN: 978-1-911687-32-0
ISBN: 978-1-911687-33-7 (ebook)

Cover and page design: Caroline Li

AMY BRADLEY
KATHERINE SEMLER

RUNNING
ON
EMPTY

NAVIGATING THE DANGERS OF
BURNOUT AT WORK

MADRID | MEXICO CITY | LONDON
BUENOS AIRES | BOGOTA | SHANGHAI

CONTENTS

For Anna, Adam, Emily and Joe
And Henry, Jackson, Mia and Oliver.

The next generation.

May they look back at this crazy time and
be thankful that they have stayed more whole.

PREFACE:
OPENING WORDS
FROM AMY

"I took this photo from our car window on a rare snow day a few weeks ago. As my husband and I drove out for an early morning run, we were met with this ethereal sight. Under an ice blue sky, hoar frost clings to branches, shining brilliant in the morning sun. Given the strict lockdown restrictions that continued in the UK, and in our keenness to get running, we didn't stop the car in this moment. Instead, I held my phone out of the passenger window and snapped this view while the car was moving.

It was only sometime later, that I realized how fleeting my appreciation of this moment had been. A snapshot, now frozen in time. Since then, this photo has become all the more poignant for me in its 'SLOW' warning for the road ahead. A reminder not to speed through life so that these moments of ephemeral beauty pass me by.

That said, my work has resumed at a blistering pace since the New Year and I have just spent nine days straight on Zoom. In recent conversations with friends, colleagues and leaders I notice an enduring theme. People talk of exhaustion; a sense of overwhelm; feelings of cynicism toward their workplaces; and crises of confidence in their ability to do a good job. What is striking about these descriptions is that they all seem to point toward the central features of burnout. So, how might these conversations reflect a wider discontent in society, brought to the fore during the pandemic and reflecting a need to change our relationship with our work?

With these questions in mind, my dear colleague Katherine and I are embarking on joint research for a new book on the phenomenon of burnout. If you are noticing any of the aspects of burnout described above or have experienced burnout and would like to join us as co-inquirers in our research, we would love to hear from you."

January 2021

Within a day of this post on LinkedIn, over 30 people had come forward from Asia, Australia, Europe, India, South Africa and the United States. Seeing the response, we realized our call for participation may have struck a chord and that we might be tapping into a pervasive and all-too-familiar current phenomenon.

CHAPTER 1

DASHBOARD
WARNING
LIGHT

When we started writing this book, we were into the third year of the COVID-19 pandemic. Within that time, we had already lived through several cycles of lockdown, been separated from our families, and seen international borders closed and reopened and then closed again. Weddings had been postponed and birthdays had been celebrated on Zoom. Millions of people were grieving loved ones whom they had lost to the virus. For our children and young people, almost four years of their educational lives have been affected in some way by the pandemic. Whether you live in Delhi, Dallas, Djibouti or Darwin, this has been a shared human experience. We have grown used to connecting with each other through phone and laptop screens or from behind face masks. This entire book project has been researched and written between us remotely. We have not met our co-contributors in person, nor have they met each other. They trusted us to share their stories from their living rooms, workplaces, kitchens and bedrooms during our weekly 'Running on Empty' virtual community calls.

With the regular commute gone for many people and no transitionary time between work and home, our physical spaces have become blurred. At the height of lockdown, we would work, eat and help our kids do their homework – all at the kitchen table – and then we would get up and do the same again the next day. No wonder reports of chronic stress and burnout appear in the press every day, with people describing themselves working longer hours, facing higher workloads, and dealing with more demands at work and at home than they have ever known before. A study on remote working, for example, found that working hours in 2020 were 30% higher than before the pandemic, with over half of those additional hours being done outside the normal working day.[1] In 2021, the American Psychological Association reported that 79% of people had experienced work-related stress that month alone.[2] Moreover, research spanning 46 countries during the pandemic suggests that 89% of people feel their work life is getting worse, with 85% of them saying their overall wellbeing has declined.[3] Job resignations in the United States in 2021 were up by 15% on 2019, which was a record year in itself.[4] It seems that the pandemic has been a catalyst for a collective awakening when it comes to reassessing our relationship with work.

It was our own contemporaneous existential work crises that brought us together to research and write. We began to surface our struggles in conversation with each other, particularly as the COVID-19 pandemic hit. So, we wondered, how might our conversation reflect a wider malaise, brought to the fore during the pandemic and reflecting a need to readdress our relationships with ourselves, each other and our work? In his collected essays, C. Wright Mills speaks of how our private troubles can reveal public issues,[5] so, with this in mind, we set about our research. By sharing our own and others' personal experiences of overwhelm and burnout in this book, our aim is to shed more light on a society-wide phenomenon that we know is complex, highly individual and deeply entrenched.

The concept of burnout has been around since the 1970s due to early work by Herbert Freudenberger[6] and then Christina Maslach;[7] however, in the wake of the COVID-19 pandemic, overwhelm and burnout have been two of the most widely covered phenomena in the popular business press. According to a May 2021 article, three out of five workers across the world say they feel burnt out, with a 2020 study claiming the figure is three in four.[8] Employees are now looking for more choice, flexibility and freedom than ever before, and statistics show that if they do not get what they want, they are prepared to vote with their feet.[9] Employers across all industries and job roles are currently facing mass resignations, with 3.6 million US workers resigning in May 2021 alone.[10] Against this backdrop, organizations are now being forced to take burnout among their workforce more seriously. In our leadership development, coaching and consulting work, we are often asked by HR professionals, leaders and managers for support. Everyone appears to be noticing that burnout is an issue, but few seem to know how to deal with it.

In this book we make a deliberate distinction between the experiences of overwhelm and burnout, as we found that our co-contributors fell into three camps: those who had experienced burnout, which was significant and debilitating enough for them to define it as a watershed moment in their lives; those who felt they were living *in* burnout when we met with them; and those who were feeling so overwhelmed with work that they felt they were teetering on the edge and were at risk of burnout. With research from 2016 suggesting that more than half of the global working population is in a state of 'overextension' when it comes to their work, this suggests that feelings of overwhelm may be a dashboard warning light for a large proportion of the global workforce. They may not yet be in burnout, but without remedial and timely action, they may soon succumb.[11]

In our initial call for participants, we had people come forward from financial services, the public sector, aviation, secondary and higher education, non-governmental organizations, consulting, retail and the technology sectors. Our co-contributors work at all levels of seniority, from front-line staff to middle managers, from leaders to CEOs, and from independent contractors to consultants.

We understood from these people that burnout is not something that can be 'overcome.' Those who have been through burnout talk about how they continue to precariously live in its shadow, knowing with a heightened sense of alertness that it might return at any time. One of our central theses in this book, therefore, is to challenge notions of 'recovery' from burnout, and we have resisted writing a self-help guide that seeks to offer people *the* answer. Despite the voracious appetite we see in our own work for tips and shortcuts, we realize how naive and wrong it would be to attempt to present neatly packaged solutions for individuals or organizations. We have come to learn that there is no silver bullet for burnout, no five steps to conquer it. Having journeyed alongside people living with or on the edge of burnout over an extended period, we have instead been able to uncover learnings, personal prevention strategies and ongoing healing practices.

This book looks at the current overwhelm and burnout crisis through a lens of discovery and seeks to highlight some of the root causes of workplace despair. Furthermore, by bringing people together into community inquiry, we aim to share a collectively imagined way ahead for organizations to tackle this pervasive phenomenon. *Running on Empty* hopes to give readers a sense of when burnout is happening or imminent, and it suggests deeply human and radical paths toward prevention and healing. We hope that leaders, managers, HR professionals, coaches and individuals alike will be touched by these stories and inspired by the healing practices we describe.

This book is structured as follows. *Chapter 2* defines overwhelm and burnout – the central concepts of the book – and sets out potential reasons for our society-wide despair when it comes to our relationship with work. We suggest that despite over half a century of research, burnout persists because of an enduring work ethic that leads us to believe that total engagement in our work is a measure of self-worth. We also suggest that a new 'labour of love' work ethic means that many people look to their work for fulfilment, friendship and even love. Burnout persists because we cling on to these ideals and fear losing the meaning that work promises. It is only when we reassess the relative importance of work in relation to other aspects of our lives that we can begin to address burnout.

In *Chapter 3*, we track our own existential work crises that brought us into this research, with 12 hours on screen becoming the norm, our to-do lists growing longer, and the pressures we felt when the boundaries blurred between home and work. It was only by disclosing our struggles to each other that we were able to build connection and understanding beyond our work, which helped us to realize we were not alone. This chapter also describes our community inquiry research process, in which we brought people together to discuss their experiences, their paths to healing and the practices that they found to be nourishing along the way.

Chapter 4 focuses on experiences of overwhelm in particular. Here, we share the experiences of three people who all found themselves perilously close to burnout at the height of the COVID-19 pandemic. Despite their work roles, industries and personal circumstances all being very different, they shared common symptoms including exhaustion, anxiety, insomnia and physical pain. By capturing these stories 'fresh' with proximity to the experiences, we aim to show how overwhelm manifests. If we see burnout on a spectrum, we suggest that overwhelm is a clear sign that people are on their way towards burnout.

By contrast, *Chapter 5* is a set of retrospective stories, with Chelsea, Sally, Dominic, Ananya and Malcolm each having suffered burnout in the past. We have lightly fictionalized these stories, adding colour and detail, to make them more vivid and experiential for the reader and to help disguise the individuals' true identities. We heard many stories of burnout during our research for this book, and the five 'songs of burnout' we chose to feature in this chapter demonstrate the complex interplay between an individual's personality, their work context and the circumstances of their personal lives that lead to the perfect storm.

Chapter 6 is a synthesis of our learning from the five songs of burnout featured in *Chapter 5*. When individuals with certain dispositions find themselves in the wrong kind of work environment, they can experience workaholism leading to exhaustion and ultimately burnout. This chapter also shows the devastating impact of overwork on the body, including impaired hormone functioning, memory loss, emotional numbness and dissociation. We also show how line managers carry a disproportionate influence when it comes to burnout, either preventing or promoting it depending on how constructive or destructive the impact of their leadership is. Finally, looking at Chelsea's, Sally's and Ananya's stories in particular, we show that experiences of burnout are not gender neutral and suggest that working mothers were at an increased risk of burnout during the pandemic.

Our research co-contributors described being profoundly changed by their experiences of burnout, so *Chapter 7* charts how many of them have found their way back to a balance that is more attuned to their needs and to the dangers that lie in excessive work. This chapter describes the practices that have helped them heal, remain healthy and continue to be self-aware in the face of work, such as meditation, mindfulness, movement, sound, making and visual art, being in nature and conversation. We discuss how these activities help people to come to know their limits better, to communicate what they will and will not do, and to shape the work conditions they need to remain whole.

In *Chapter 8*, we share our co-contributors' vision of a future where organizations are radically reimagined to put an end to burnout. In this envisaged future, we demand different working conditions, with employees and employers co-creating a shared idea of what it means to lead a healthy work life and how work fits into a life well lived. Workplace cultures are based on dignity and fairness as universal rights rather than contingent rewards; compassion for self and for others is prioritized, even at the expense of productivity; and purpose is seen to come from leisure and not from work.

We draw the book to a close by stating that one thing is certain: we will not eradicate burnout alone. Individuals, organizations and societies will all need to play their part to move us beyond self-interest and towards reciprocity and collective action in order to design future workplaces for the benefit of all.

CHAPTER 2

LOOKING FOR LOVE IN ALL THE WRONG PLACES

"THE CIRCUMSTANCES THAT PROMOTE DESPAIR – AND POTENTIALLY THEREFORE ADDICTION- ARE, WITH EACH DECADE, MORE AND MORE ENTRENCHED IN THE INDUSTRIALIZED WORLD, FROM THE EAST TO THE WEST: MORE ISOLATION AND LONELINESS, LESS COMMUNAL CONTACT, MORE STRESS, MORE ECONOMIC INSECURITY, MORE FEAR."[12]

GABOR MATÉ, 2018

In our work roles, we had begun to notice ourselves repeatedly bearing witness to individual suffering. In sessions we were each facilitating, leaders would dutifully show up on Zoom, yet with a collective lethargy that leaked through the screen. We began to notice similar accounts being reported in the business press.[13] People were present but absent, looking joyless and beaten down. With over 90% of the global working population living in countries with some form of workplace closure at that time,[14] it was not surprising that we would hear accounts of people struggling. One leader, for example, spoke of having seven family members in her apartment, having taken her husband's brother and his children into their home while her sister-in-law was hospital-ized with COVID-19. She talked of an overwhelming sense of responsibility to look after them all while also trying to juggle her work and feeling that she was failing on all fronts. With one in ten Europe-ans now living alone,[15] accounts of isolation and loneliness were also prevalent. One of the youngest leaders we worked with during the pandemic spoke about being single, without children and confined to working from his studio apartment in Italy throughout the lockdowns. In a session together, he realized that we were the first people he had spoken to in over a week.

As human beings, we are social animals. What drives us is to feel we belong, to have nurturing rela-tionships, and to sense that we are valued, appre-ciated and respected.[16] Many of us look to have our social needs met from our workplaces, yet during the pandemic the very thing we craved was unavailable. We know from prior research that three work-related factors can lead to stress – uncertainty, lack of information and loss of control[17] – and we had these in spades during the pandemic. During a coaching session, one manager admitted to feeling completely expendable:

"Everyone is feeling insecure. People are being let go because of the downturn, but no one knows who will be next in line. I feel completely untethered."

Around 114 million jobs were lost globally in 2020,[18] which was four times higher than during the global financial crisis of 2009. No wonder so many people began to overwork to try and prove their worth. COVID-19 was a recipe for addiction – a Molotov cocktail of isolation, powerlessness and stress.

Research suggests that almost half of the US working population now consider themselves workaholics, with the main indicators of workaholism being checking your phone while in bed or at weekends, worrying about work on days off and feeling too busy to take a vacation.[19] Surely, these descriptors are the norm for most working professionals today, so no wonder many of us come to a point where we hit a wall. As a leading psychiatrist says, "Because we are so stretched and have experienced chronic stress for so long, we have zero margin for error."[20]

With so much talk of overwork, exhaustion, feelings of cynicism and personal crises of confidence, what was striking about the accounts we were hearing was that they seemed to point toward the central features of burnout.[21] The idea of burnout is not new. It was first described in 1974 by Herbert Freudenberger, who worked in the treatment of substance abuse and with drug abuse training programmes. It was his work in free clinics and therapeutic communities that led him to develop the clinical concept of burnout.[22] The word itself calls up a striking image suggesting that if we give too much to our work, in the end our spark will go out – we will be spent, hollow and empty.

Burnout has since been regarded as a work-related syndrome that is not just confined to the helping professions (such as nursing). Thousands of studies have been conducted since its inception across job roles and industry sectors, and it is commonly agreed that burnout happens when we experience three specific things: exhaustion, cynicism toward our work and an ongoing sense of reduced personal accomplishment.[23] Exhaustion relates to experiences of chronic stress over time. Cynicism involves becoming cold, detached and sceptical about our job or workplace; we experience ourselves as robotic and lose the human element when dealing with customers and colleagues, and even in our relationships at home. Reduced personal accomplishment relates to negative feelings towards ourselves in terms of our ability and capacity to do our job. According to this definition of burnout, it is only when we experience all three states simultaneously that we are classed as burnt out.

It is important to make this distinction, since it has been argued that burnout is too often used as a synonym for 'tired' and that we are not in fact living through a burnout epidemic – what we are seeing is simply a case of overdiagnosis.[24] Research suggests that according to this three-factor definition of burnout, 20% of the working population currently have a profile consistent with burnout. That said, the two leading researchers in the field, Michael Leiter and Christina Maslach, have found that all three qualities of burnout are on the rise among the working population. Their research has found that more than 50% of people are 'overextended,' 'ineffective' and 'disengaged,' which means that over half of the working population may not yet be burnt out but are certainly on their way.[25] In our research for this book, we also began to see burnout on a spectrum, with some of our co-contributors describing themselves as on route to burnout, which we term 'overwhelmed.' Whereas other co-contributors recounted traumatic and visceral lived experiences of burnout comprising total physical, mental and emotional shutdown.

Burnout can be defined as a mismatch between expectations and reality when it comes to a person and their job.[26] This mismatch may be related to **workload** (e.g. having too many targets and deadlines combined with not enough resources to do the job); **control** (e.g. being micromanaged or feeling a lack of autonomy or influence); **reward** (e.g. not feeling valued, appreciated or fairly rewarded for our efforts); **community** (e.g. feeling isolated from others, or experiencing instances of interpersonal conflict, disrespect or incivility at work); **fairness** (e.g. experiencing discrimination or favouritism); and **values** (e.g. continually being asked to do work that appears pointless, or experiencing a disconnect between our own values, motivations and ideals and those espoused and demonstrated within the organization). As Maslach and Leiter clarify:

"Burnout is not a problem of individuals but of the social environment in which they work. Workplaces shape how people interact with one another and how they carry out their jobs. When the workplace does not recognize the human side of work, and there are major mismatches between the nature of the job and the nature of people, there will be a greater risk of burnout."[27]

Of the above six areas, fairness has been found to be the most important factor in predicting burnout among people who score high in one of the three areas (exhaustion, cynicism and reduced personal accomplishment) a year beforehand.[28] In one study, employees experiencing high levels of cynicism were more likely to reengage with their work if they felt their organization communicated with them well and kept them in the loop about important developments.[29] Workplace relationships have been found to be key to exacerbating or alleviating burnout, particularly the quality of the relationship between line manager and direct report and the quality of relationships between colleagues. As we know, people seek to belong, to be nurtured and to be respected within their workplace – and the extent to which our relationships meet or thwart these motivations has been found to relate to burnout.[30] Furthermore, research has suggested a link between leadership behaviours and the exacerbation or alleviation of burnout, with experiences of bullying, aggression or abuse from leaders, or indeed the reverse – that is to say, inaction or the turning of a blind eye to toxic behaviours – also being linked to burnout.[31]

Maslach and her colleagues have developed one of the most well-known measures of burnout – the Maslach Burnout Inventory – and they suggest that experiencing one or two of the dimensions is a risk factor. As described earlier in this chapter, it is only when all three are combined that a person is likely to be pushed into burnout.[32] One of the problems with conceiving burnout through such predictors and measures is that it ends up suggesting a binary 'all or nothing' view. We are either burnt out or we are not. However, in listening to people's stories in the course of our research for this book, it was clear that individuals were living through a profound and in many ways traumatic experience. If we went by measures alone, they might not have qualified as burnt out; however, they knew their experience showed something was profoundly wrong in their relationship with work.

Over the course of our research, we have also come to understand that experiences of burnout are highly individual and highly contextual. We see these experiences at one end of a continuum with flourishing at the other. For some, burnout equates to total and utter shutdown. These people are barely able to function in their daily lives. Others experience many of the symptoms of burnout but somehow manage to keep going. We have also come to understand, particularly in light of the pandemic, that overwhelm lies somewhere on this continuum: your fuel gauge is running low, a dashboard warning light on the road to burnout. Among all of the stories of burnout we heard, one thing was common: the experience was significant enough for people to feel that it was a watershed moment in their lives. In many ways, their accounts matched what certain scholars define as a traumatic experience.[33]

Despite half a century of research, burnout remains endemic, some say because there are no universally agreed symptoms; others argue that there is a lack of consensus on how long symptoms should persist before someone is classed as burnt out; and others believe there is a lack of agreement on the ultimate consequences of burnout on a person's work and home life.[34] Writing in 2014, Leiter, Arnold Bakker and Maslach state: "Despite reasoned and impassioned calls for action, progress has been modest."[35]

More recently, writers have suggested that burnout persists for reasons that run deep into the heart of our societal consciousness – for example, in some parts of our world, in an enduring Protestant work ethic. In this case, the belief is that hard work is a route to making oneself a good person who will eventually be rewarded in heaven for their efforts. This pervasive belief – and others like it – can lead to total engagement in work, with burnout being the ultimate sacrifice. Alternatively, authors such as Sarah Jaffe argue that a new 'labour of love' work ethic has replaced the Protestant work ethic in much of the Western world in the post-industrial era. She writes:

"Today's workers are cheery and 'flexible,' net-worked and net-savvy, creative and caring. ... Their hours stretch long and the lines between the home and the workplace blurs. Security, the watchword of the industrial ethic, where workers spent a lifetime at one job and earned a pension on their way out the door, has been traded for fulfilment. And the things we used to keep for ourselves – indeed, the things the industrial workplace wanted to minimize – are suddenly in demand on the job, including friendships, our feelings and our love."[36]

In this vein, perhaps one of the reasons burnout continues unabated is the emphasis we place on the role of work in our lives. We mistakenly look to our work as the source of all our fulfilment – "a means not just to a paycheck but to dignity, character and a sense of purpose."[37] Burnout persists because we cling to these ideals and fear losing the meaning that work promises. It is only when we reassess the importance of work in relation to other aspects of our lives that we can begin to address burnout.

Burnout may have become a cultural buzzword to line the pockets of consultants, self-helpers and the wellness industry, a product of neocapitalism, where the profit motive leads employers to put more and more demands on workers, which in turn increases stress.[38] Articles in the popular press advise us on how to battle it,[39] beat it[40] or banish it.[41] We are even given advice on how to find its cures.[42] In this book we have resisted neatly packaged solutions. Instead, our hope is that in meeting our co-inquirers' stories with humanity and compassion, we might begin to uncover the conditions that bind us – and, in doing so, understand not only how to prevent our own burnout but also how we might prevent each other's.

CHAPTER 3

OUR STORIED LIVES

In November 2021, I (Katherine) decided to move out of the city to a patch of farmland over an hour away. My children were what we call 'bungee-gone': all four were either studying or working somewhere else in the world, but vacations, unemployment, break-ups, boredom, and even laundry or a hankering for home-made lasagne would cause the bungee cord to contract and bring them back for a short while. Long live the bungee, we say! Especially during the COVID-19 restrictions and strict lockdowns in 2020, these bungee visits were a welcome comfort amid the turbulence.

Moving is notoriously stressful, especially when the move is not just around the corner but to an entirely new way of life. Far from friends, who could not travel to visit due to the restrictions, and separated from familiar things – neighbourhood shops and cafés, exercise routes, favourite restaurants, to name a few – I was feeling the sort of soul-warp that sometimes happens when we take a long-haul flight. It does not seem possible that I can enjoy coffee in the morning in Barcelona and by the afternoon be meeting and greeting participants arriving for a course in Argentina when it is still daylight, on the same day on planet Earth! My soul might be hovering somewhere over the Azores, sniffing for a trace of my trajectory.

The intensity of my work at the time of my move to the countryside was palpable. Twelve-hour days on screen were the norm, with rare stolen breaks, my to-do list growing longer every day. I was beginning every meeting with an apology for being late and there was a general lack of attention in myself and those around me to the fact that everyone was becoming exhausted, the pressure was rising and the holidays were not close enough to hold on to for hope. I told Amy on a Zoom call that I was feeling overwhelmed and Amy's face changed. We looked at each other, all those miles away, one in the UK and one in Spain, and we read the same sadness and relief in each other's eyes – sad because we saw our own exhaustion reflected in the other and relief because it could be shared and named.

REFLECTION #1: By disclosing our struggles with work partners, we can build connection and understanding beyond the work task and help ourselves to realize we are not alone.

There it was: we were both teetering on the edge of burnout, like so many others around us whom we were tasked to somehow help. But how could we help our clients, our colleagues and even our children and partners, if we ourselves could not find a solid footing?

From the sadness and relief arose a question: What was happening to us and to countless others in this vortex and how could we come together to understand and heal?

We began sharing our own stories and then the stories of others. For example, Amy had spoken to a woman who was feeling pressure to perform while working remotely in the highly emotional and relational field of special needs education. She had no opportunities to discuss challenges with colleagues in the hallways and no acknowledgement from management about the added difficulty of trying to support vulnerable young people via a computer screen. She was also living with the added stress of supporting a partner who was out of work and struggling with his mental health. I was coaching someone whose relationships with her husband, close friends and family were breaking down because all her emotional energy was going into sustaining remote work with her team, who were under extreme pressure to deliver results – and this after many months of a delayed promotion that now seemed to be an empty promise. Later, a mutual acquaintance spoke to us both about his pre-COVID-19 burnout and his long, slow road to healing and re-entry into an organization that assumed that once he was 'cured' it would be business as usual (he stepped down from his leadership position as a result).

The frequency of such cases in our conversations both privately and in our work led us to imagine a community inquiry in which we would bring people together to discuss their experiences of overwhelm or burnout, their paths to healing and the practices that they had found to be nourishing along the way. We put out a call for inquiry partners across our networks and via LinkedIn and, as described in the opening words from Amy, we received numerous responses. Some people were in the midst of burnout, some were in the process of healing, and some were coaches and counsellors who were themselves surrounded and overwhelmed by people whom they wanted to help.

We started by holding 30-minute interviews with 20 individuals who brought a variety of lenses to the topic of burnout. Touching and inspiring stories arose from every conversation. For example, a pilot had been forced to stop flying temporarily and had eventually left the profession due to work pressures, difficult shift patterns and the added stress he felt when his grown-up twin children both left home in relatively short succession. In another interview, a university professor talked about going through the motions of teaching, using visualization to imagine her audience when her students refused to turn on their cameras in their now fully online course. One of our co-inquirers who had once loved his job was feeling the cynicism of his employer, who had made him the 'last man standing' in a firm gone bankrupt, tasking him with terminating relationships and contracts until he got down to the last one, his own.

From these stories, we created two distinct groups for our co-inquiry: one for people at risk, who felt they were slipping into dangerous territory regarding overwhelm and burnout; and another group of people who were in burnout at the time or had healed from a diagnosed case of burnout. Each group was invited to a series of six 90-minute sessions over six weeks in which we provided a virtual space for them to connect, share their stories, exchange various restorative practices that were helping to sustain them at the time or had done so in the past, and engage in some in-session practices to then provide feedback. We will share our insights from these two community inquiries in *Chapter 8*.

In a parallel thread of research, we conducted individual 'burnout story' sessions, in which we dove deep into each person's account of burnout using the Biographic Narrative Interpretive Method.[43] We invited people to tell their story to one or both of us, on camera, without interruption, for as long they wanted to talk. A second phase of this method gave way to a few questions that deepened the conversation in key areas. There was so much richness in these stories that we have recounted them in fictionalized form (with the consent of the contributors of the stories) in *Chapter 5*. We have affectionately labelled them 'songs' in the tradition of orally transmitted popular epic poems, to honour the oral narrative method that we used. Through them, we aim to paint scenes that will resonate and last in our collective memory as poignant examples of the current wave of suffering that is threatening our health and happiness.

The desire to construct narratives of our lives is one of the basic schematic structures of human thought.[44] Talking about difficult life experiences enables us to make sense of them and to communicate their meanings to others.[45] So, this is a book of stories. In his work *Homo Deus*, Yuval Noah Harari narrates a history of humankind that holds our ability to create and believe in stories as the single attribute that differentiates us from all other species.[46] The 'intersubjective belief' is, in Harari's view, the secret of human domination over all other forms of life on our planet – and, indeed, perhaps our eventual demise across the whole planet. Because we are able to imagine and express stories about things that do not actually exist (such as gods, money, countries and companies), we are able to organize massive numbers of people around far-reaching ideas and ideals that we are willing to live and die for:

"Sapiens rule the world because only they can weave an intersubjective web of meaning: a web of laws, forces, entities and places that exist purely in their common imagination. This web allows humans alone to organize crusades, socialist revolutions and human rights movements."[47]

Because stories are central to our humanity, we would like to offer a storied account to sit alongside the scientific accounts of burnout, some of which we reference and which have helped us to understand this territory. It is our hope that the stories in this book, all based on real cases and fictionalized to a degree, will help you to navigate the dangers of burnout. As Harari says:

"If we want to understand our future, cracking genomes and crunching numbers is hardly enough. We must also decipher the fictions that give meaning to the world."[48]

My own story of near burnout began in those weeks after I moved to the country. My decline found fodder in the intensity and pressure of a work environment that had not previously encountered the challenges of the limitless productivity of remote working. As in most compelling plots, there was a confluence of evils. I recall stepping out onto cold, stiff grass in my socks and forcing myself to breathe the cool November air for a few seconds before lunging into my next video call. My mind lagged slightly behind the words being spoken, even my own, making it an effort to find meaning. By contrast, every morning at 3 am for weeks, I lay awake for hours; worries about tasks and projects, children, profession, relationships, future, past, present, money, health – all raced with feline agility through my mind and body. The total disconnection with myself seems so apparent now. I recall being exhausted physically and mentally yet unable to find sleep. My disconnection with others was growing as I became inwardly focused on my survival, my work, my lack of sleep, my obsession, my dysfunction, my... my... I felt guilty about working too hard and guilty about not meeting expectations on all fronts. I neglected exercise and proper meals, willpower gone, except for the obsessive drive to get it all done on the work front. Mission impossible.

Enter this project, and perspective and connection crept back. First there was the moment of realization with Amy, then the conversations with her and others, the interviews, the community inquiry. This was a path to health again, through many different elements, all of which came to light in the contributions of our co-inquirers.

REFLECTION #2: Overwhelmed and destabilized both at home and at work, burnout can feel perilously close. If one of these areas remains balanced and stable, it may help to sustain us in the other.

The people who have brought their stories and practices to this book come from a wide range of backgrounds, professions, locations and beliefs. We are deeply grateful to each of them for contributing their stories, their insights and their practices. For the sake of anonymity, we have changed the names of all people and organizations in this book.

We heard stories from a number of people in the course of our research and have focused specifically on eight of them. **Igor** is the dean of a college who, as its leader, found himself in the eye of the storm during the pandemic. Feeling everyone in the organization was looking to him for clarity and answers, Igor found himself crumbling under the immense pressure. **Pierre** found himself being made redundant within three months of moving from the UK to Australia to take on a new work role. Feeling worthless, alone and far from friends and family, Pierre's mental, physical and emotional health began to suffer. Working in the retail industry, **Brian** had been tipped for a board-level position. However, in 2020 he found himself in uncharted territory that became quickly unnavigable. Having been promoted a year earlier, he had moved roles and teams and he was now being asked to make people redundant due to a restructure. Work pressures alongside the death of his father earlier that year meant that Brian was struggling to cope. **Chelsea's** difficult marriage and a chronically ill child did not initially affect her ability to work at top standards in a complex international non-governmental organization, but it all caught up with her and she began to suffer from serious memory loss. **Dominic** experienced burnout several years ago, having been slowly let down and traumatized working in financial services. He resigned and left the industry to become an actor, and began to build a new career. **Ananya** is a health and wellbeing coach and was transferred to a new and exciting part of her consulting firm just before COVID-19, only to find herself working in a system that did not value her strengths. She felt lost and isolated and unable to meet the overwhelming demands of her new position. **Malcolm** lives with his wife and family in Singapore. His burnout experience started five years prior, when he was working in a leadership role for a family-owned multinational. Becoming consumed by work demands and the desire to do a good job, Malcolm found himself sacrificing his own values and needs in service of the organization. **Sally** experienced burnout three years prior to our research while working as a HR director. Reporting to an abusive boss, she found herself being increasingly undermined and bullied. In a hierarchal and patriarchal environment in which she felt she had no voice or safe space to speak up, the toxicity of Sally's work culture eventually led to her burnout.

Our co-inquiry groups contained **Mario**, who was out of work at the time. He struggled with his mental health and with the fact that his wife, **Helene**, was feeling exhausted and overwhelmed. Helene works with children who have special needs. She used to support children in school, but during the pandemic she met them online. Many of them were suffering far more than they used to. Both Helene and Mario live and work at home, and were confined by COVID-19 restrictions at the time of the co-inquiry sessions and were unsure how to support each other. **Terry** is a university professor who, during the global pandemic, faced the difficulty and stress of teaching students online who were themselves struggling with mental health challenges. According to Terry, the university's senior management was incapable of seeing or supporting faculty with the additional challenges of teaching online. **Mason** is a mergers and acquisitions specialist who was rapidly promoted by his CEO, only to find himself tasked with saving small pieces of the ship as it sank. During the pandemic, he went from being passionate about the company to hating his job and his bosses. **Hattie** worked for one of the largest global tech companies and found herself questioning the value and purpose of her job in the light of the pandemic. In her mid-fifties, **Britta** had just quit her job as a chief marketing officer. After spending years working longer and longer hours and feeling increasing pressure to be 'always on,' she decided to step away from corporate life.

Our intention is to shine light on the issues that are leading people to suffer, while exploring healing practices, both preventively and to be used in the wake of overwhelm and burnout. Our hope is to contribute to a healthier world, in which fulfilment is compassionate, multifaceted and nuanced rather than tending toward the obsessive, addictive and all-consuming approaches that we have seen in our own practices, in our colleagues and loved ones, and in our research.

REFLECTION #3: The growth and prosperity of mega-organizations is dependent on diminishing returns for workers, creating ever-increasing pressure on individuals to produce more and more. At a time when sustainability is becoming a critical factor for companies, the pursuit of ever-increasing growth needs to be checked by the fact that organizations can only be as sustainable as their leaders and workers are.

Economist Jan Eeckhout has written about how the current unprecedented prosperity and wild success of the businesses that define our era are threatening the essence of work.[49] He calls this the "profit paradox" and his book by this title got us wondering about the human experience of the destruction of work. Could this be a cause of the burnout pandemic we are seeing? Have we gone down a path that sustains the quest for growth for organizations but makes our own personal sustainability impossible? We will discuss some of Eeckhout's suggestions and bring his economic analysis into dialogue alongside the stories of our co-contributors in this work.

CHAPTER 4

LOST
AT SEA

"SOMETHING IS GOING ON – I KNOW IT ISN'T GOOD, BUT IS IT BURNOUT?"

PIERRE, RESEARCH CO-CONTRIBUTOR

In our research for this book, we have come to understand that burnout is elusive and difficult to pin down. Everyone's experience is different. There are multiple routes to burnout. Individuals endure varying symptoms, and, in burnout's aftermath, each person has to learn how to heal in their own way. That said, we are coming to realize, particularly in the light of the pandemic, that there are warning signs that signal our tanks are running on empty. In the hope of catching a glimpse of these warning signs, we gathered stories from three people who all found themselves walking toward burnout at the height of COVID-19. As one of them said when we convened on Zoom:

"I'm holding on, just holding on. Stopping myself from going over that boundary. It's an exhausting place to be. I'm conscious of trying to stop myself going over the edge."

With struggles converging in their personal and professional lives, at the same time as they were trying to navigate challenges brought about by the pandemic, Pierre, Igor and Brian all found themselves "lost at sea," in Igor's words, and during "a perfect storm," as described by Brian. For Pierre, the feeling that he was "going under" came from the combination of being made redundant within a few months of moving with his wife and baby from the UK to Australia; having no access to furlough during the pandemic because of his temporary visa status; and the death of a lifelong friend thousands of miles away. Igor said he was experiencing an "oceanic" sense of responsibility as dean of a college, when, at the start of the pandemic, he perceived everyone in the organization was looking to him for answers. Brian, a senior leader within the retail sector in the UK, described how changing work roles, taking on a new team, and his father's terminal illness and subsequent death during lockdown combined to form the "collision" that led to a sense of total overwhelm.

This chapter is a snapshot of stories told at a particular moment in history, when three individuals found themselves living on the edge of burnout during a global pandemic. When we met on Zoom, they talked with such immediacy about their experiences they helped us to better appreciate the signs of burnout. We know experiences of burnout are highly individual and highly contextual; however, in hearing Pierre's, Igor's and Brian's stories, there are clear commonalities. As we said in *Chapter 1*, it is our hope that by capturing these stories 'fresh' with proximity to the experiences, we might understand overwhelm as a warning sign. Why? Because those people who are on the other side of burnout explained how they did not see it coming. It was only with hindsight that they could see all the signs were there, but they somehow ignored or suppressed them because their inner voices about needing to work hard were louder than the voices that said, "slow down, take it easy, take care of yourself." The stories in *Chapter 5* are therefore told through the rear-view mirror based on individuals looking back on their experiences with the benefit of hindsight. But here, in this chapter, we felt it equally important to capture the here and now, by gathering insights from people experiencing overwhelm particularly because, as we have learned from those who look back at burnout, there is no such thing as 'recovery.' Instead, these people live with greater insight into its signs while knowing that the spectre of burnout is ever present. It follows them wherever they go and lurks in the shadows waiting for a moment to creep up on them once more.

AN ASSAULT
ON THE BODY
AND MIND

The physical signs were the first hint that something was awry. Igor noticed a "clutching sensation" at the top of his stomach. He had experienced the same sensation before during periods in his career, but not for such a sustained amount of time. It was as though he had been punched so hard, the wind had been knocked out of him. This feeling had been constant for 12 months. Despite being gripped by enduring anxiety, he perceived that the demands of his job as the leader of an organization outweighed the compassion that he owed to himself. "What am I going to do? I've got a job to do," he thought.

Burnout is known to start with exhaustion.[50] Faced with the relentlessness of work (in Igor's and Brian's cases) or the relentless search for work (in Pierre's case), exhaustion set in for all three. Igor said:

"It's just work, work, work. So that's exhausting. ... Everyone wants a piece of me, there's no transition space. So, I'm leaving one meeting and immediately going on to another meeting and having to be on my game immediately. Sometimes I just feel like I've been beaten up at the end of the day."

Another physical sign that burnout was perilously close was that each of them began to have trouble sleeping. They'd had no problems sleeping in the past, yet now insomnia had taken hold. Igor described how, like clockwork, every single morning he would wake up at 4 am and his brain would immediately switch on like a lightbulb. Work would begin going round and round in his head. Once awake, he could not switch off. Brian describes being physically exhausted yet hyper-alert:

"I wasn't sleeping. I was constantly thinking about work and my family, and by the same token, I was permanently exhausted."

Feeling exhausted and sleep deprived, Brian was becoming increasingly irritable at work and the smallest of things would set him off. He became openly impatient and short tempered with colleagues, particularly if he felt that their work was not up to scratch. His expectations became more and more unreasonable, and he lost the ability to empathize:

"I'd say, "How is it so difficult for you to be able to do simple things?" Forgetting that they are fresh-faced and out of university. They've been working for six months and don't have much experience."

We know that sleep and rest are not the same. They go hand in hand to ensure we are completely regenerated and restored, so the exhaustion Pierre, Igor and Brian were each experiencing became magnified because of a lack of rest in all aspects of their lives (e.g. physically, mentally, emotionally and sensorily).[51] Igor reflected on how his life had become endlessly active and at the same time deeply dissatisfying:

"I get up, come into the office, often I'm back-to-back on Teams from 8.30 am to 6.30 pm without a break, exhausted, then straight into family life, no transition into family life, cook, eat, bed, get up, Teams, eat, sleep. I survive through to a weekend where I'm completely knackered until Sunday morning and then I'm back into preparing for Monday. For me it's like, what are you doing? This is not how I want to live my life."

The toll on Pierre's body was becoming so great that he became crippled with back pain. After sitting at his computer for hours and days upon end, in a relentless search for work, he had given himself a slipped disc:

"The body was speaking to me in its own way and there was nothing I could do but listen to that because it was bloody painful."

Their bodies were speaking to them through physical pain, but the critical voices in their minds seemed to be speaking louder. When we feel threatened, the part of our brain that registers danger kicks in, and cortisol and adrenaline are released so that we are ready to fight, fly or freeze.[52] When this response turns inward toward ourselves, the fight response becomes self-criticism, the flight response becomes withdrawal and the freeze response becomes rumination.[53] Following prolonged stress and pressure both at home and at work, Pierre, Igor and Brian each talked in their own ways about turning inwards and becoming highly self-critical. They also talked about an overriding desire to withdraw, hide or run away, and they spoke of endlessly ruminating about work. For example, Igor said:

"The voice in my head is going, 'You're lucky to have a job.' I feel guilty that I get paid an awful lot of money to suck it up and deal with it. There are lots of other people in worse situations than me and my team needs me. 'What are you doing? Why are you thinking in that way? Grow up!'"

LIVING TRAUMA

As we listened to Brian, Pierre and Igor speak, we noticed how each of them framed their experiences in traumatic terms, if we understand trauma to be an experience that is significant enough to shatter the foundations upon which our views of ourselves and the world are based. As scholar Ronnie Janoff-Bulman describes them, "traumas are shocks to our inner worlds."[54] Igor, for example, framed his experience terms of physical trauma: "I feel dislocated and fractured." Pierre, on the other hand, described himself as mentally "in pieces." Surrounded by pain, upset and death at the height of the pandemic, alongside the stress and pressure in their work lives, for all three cortisol and adrenaline filled their bodies and their lives became about survival. For each of them, it appears to have been a case of existing from day to day with their most primitive instincts kicking in in the face of threat. They were in fight, flight or freeze mode. Pierre said he "felt like running away, just legging it," whereas Brian talked about wanting to "curl up into a ball, put the duvet over my head and shut the outside world out." Igor's "oceanic" sense of overwhelm made him want to "hide away." He said, "I just wanted it to stop. It became too much and

I couldn't deal with it." During this time, all three found it difficult to do anything other than live, eat and sleep, although even that goal became futile. As Brian said, "I just wanted to eat or sleep and could basically do neither."

Their distress was so pronounced that they appeared to display some of the common symptoms of post-traumatic stress disorder (PTSD).[55] Brian in particular talked about becoming incapable of making the simplest of decisions:

"[Take] something as simple as "What do you want for supper?" You can't ask me that question because I can't cope with giving you an answer."

He found himself becoming so stressed that in an attempt to bring some control to a world that was otherwise in disarray, he would become obsessive:

"If the tins weren't in the right place or the towels weren't ordered, I would go into meltdown, like my brain had regressed to being a toddler and I couldn't emotionally cope with anything."

By contrast, in the course of our conversation and despite living through "some of the darkest days" he ever had, Igor realized that he had not cried in over a year. Brian said his "emotional temperature switch was turned off completely." So numbed were his feelings that, on the day of his father's funeral, Brian was back in the office "operating as normal" two hours after the service.

On top of the pandemic, 2020 saw global political instability, the killing of George Floyd and subsequent protests across the world, which for Brian led to sensory overload. He talked about having to sit in a darkened room at the end of a work day in an attempt to cope, to try to remove any external stimulus:

"It gets to the stage where I can't cope with too much stimulus and my other half, she'll be lying on the sofa and she'll occasionally knock the remote control on the floor and we've got wooden floors, and it makes a sort of clattering noise and I'll be irrationally angry as a result and I can't relax for a long time afterwards. It takes me quite a long time for my heart rate to return to normal."

Igor, Brian and Pierre all threw themselves deeper and deeper into work as a means of distraction. Pierre noticed an unhelpful overdrive that kicked in for him at this time:

"I had this constant feeling that I had to find the answer to make all this stuff right. It was a constant gnawing away at me to find the magic solution and to make all this work, and that created a huge amount of fatigue. It was causing me physical trauma. If you could use that word. Trauma to the back."

Later in the interview, he talked further about how his industriousness was becoming his source of destruction because he would "keep going and going and going relentlessly in order to try and make it right." Igor eventually started to witness himself going into total shutdown:

"Maybe my system has gone into protective mode like when your MacBook has too many apps open, it shuts down. That's what it feels like. I've shut down."

As this chapter has hopefully shown, we met Brian, Igor and Pierre in the thick of it. They courageously related their stories to us in real time, as each of them was holding on for dear life to try to prevent themselves from falling into the abyss. By contrast, the next chapter is a set of retrospective stories, with each of our co-contributors having experienced burnout in the past. That said, for many, it appears to have been as raw and real as if they were still experiencing it.

CHAPTER 5

FIVE
SONGS OF
BURNOUT

CHELSEA

CHELSEA moved from the United States to the Netherlands with her husband in the early 2000s. Their son was born shortly after their relocation, and as an infant he was diagnosed with a life-limiting illness. Chelsea works full time as a senior manager in an international non-governmental organization. We spoke with her in May 2021, just over a year into the COVID-19 pandemic.

My son was in and out of the hospital throughout his early childhood, but especially intensely the year he turned six. The nurse on the ward where they kept my son was the first to confront me. "How dare she?" I thought. What does she know about me? "You're not having a normal reaction to this," she said in a confidential tone, her voice even quieter than when she had told me the week before that they had to do another round of aggressive cortisone medication for my son's bowels. She tucked her chin under and rolled her eyes up to look at me. "You've been here two weeks, racing back and forth from work, perfect hair and make-up, and you've shown no emotion.

It's the same reaction whether I tell you he is doing well or that he has responded badly to something. We're just not used to seeing parents not cry or show some emotion." What did she want from me? I am strong. I am being strong, just like everyone at work says I am. I can power through. And if I don't, I will be letting people down. She's probably thinking I didn't take care of myself when I was pregnant. My husband also said as much. Should I have had that extra vitamin? Should I have stopped working earlier on?

Mum calls: "Everything is great, Mum. All good. Another round of medication coming, but work is fine and Danny should be able to come home next week."

"I would not be doing that well," she says. "I am not doing that well, and it has to be a lot less stressful for me than it is for you," she adds.

I used to play guitar. I stopped because the callouses on my fingers made it feel strange to type. I feel the callous with my thumb, rubbing it as I try to remember where my office is. I walk out into the large main lobby on my way to a meeting, but I have forgotten my notebook. I will need it to take notes. But now ... where was my office? I know it has a yellow sign with my name on it. I was just there. But which direction? I can't be lost like this in the middle of the building. There's Lars. He wants to ask me something.

"Hi, Lars. Yes, I am headed to a meeting, but I forgot something. So, if you walk me to my office we can talk on the way."

Lars starts walking straight ahead.

"You know where my office is?" I ask, trying to sound light and jovial.

"Well, I usually see you coming out of the west hall-way, so ..."

And then it all comes back to me. Past the reception area, then the news stand and down the west hallway on the left. Saved.

My son, home from the hospital now, picks up the home phone. "I'll give you five euros if you know our address, I tell him." 52 Margrietstraat. Of course. I leave the parking lot and take a left. No need for Google Maps. I remember now.

I went to the doctor, expecting they would find a neu-rological disease or worse – a tumour, brain cancer, something irreparable. I feared the long slow months of steadily getting worse. They found nothing wrong with my brain. The story was in my blood. I had none of the good things: my vitamins, minerals, white cell count and everything else that should have been there were completely depleted. And I had loads of all the bad things: cortisol, cholesterol, anaemia, thyroid imbalance, the list goes on.

"I don't know how you are functioning," the doctor said, staring through me before he wrote a prescription for supplements. "I don't know why you're not telling me that you are suffering physical and mental burnout."

"Because I'm not," I answered. "I'm fine."

And so, he recommended therapy. Same thing there: how was I not acknowledging my fatigue? "You have completely dissociated yourself from what your body and mind are feeling. You risk developing multiple personalities, because you have been so good at compartmentalizing all the aspects of your life."

Suddenly I could feel this threat. How would I be strong if I could not control whether I was me or another me at any given moment? Whom would I get in each situation? How could I keep my work up to snuff? My hands tingled at the thought of colleagues seeing me flounder – not making sense, can't rely on her, strange looks in the hallways – and then my boss would notice. A dread that reminded me of the paralysing childhood fear that my mother was dead in a car crash whenever she was ten minutes late to pick me up. Eyes blinking back tears until she walked through the vine-covered gate of the schoolyard. Those were the longest minutes I knew.

It was mid-December when a tingling dread took hold. Limbs heavy and clumsy and partly numb. One morning I went to work, sat down and started crying. I couldn't stop. I had to leave. I took the bus home and cried on the bus. I cried at home, Danny looking on, quiet, sweet, wondering. Everything I did for a few days would bring on tears, so I gave in. I slept for two weeks, still checking emails from my bed, before I felt ready to move about, go out onto the patio, play with my son. I miss the numbness sometimes but not the crying. Achy loneliness was the first thing I felt when the tingling wore off.

My husband had gone to Portugal for a work opportunity, but we both knew his choice was to move away from pain and toward some sunny sense of hope. I didn't miss him specifically, really, but felt that special aloneness of taking care of a child and not having someone notice the goings on or talk to me or even disagree. The sun was my only solace. It was a warm spell in Holland and I regained the strength to get out of bed. I would sit out on the patio while my son played and feel the warmth on my skin. Frothy coffee and sunshine became my balm. Only in short bursts. I treasured this comfort.

I never did switch off from the machine of work, churning audibly in my head. I tapped into the goings on in the office and with clients, but with a detachment now, a focus on the task that felt like blinders. The support from colleagues felt overly sweet, like a cheap dessert, made to convey pleasure fast but not to last. It left me feeling cheated when Emma called with her fake empathy: "I wanted to check and see how you're doing. We miss you around here." She spoke quickly, perhaps trying to get the conversation over with. "There has been so much going on, I would have called sooner but I thought you might need some space" – she paused, but not long enough for me to feel invited to speak – "so I thought I would call and give you an update on people and the things that are going on. Did you hear that Johannes moved to Julia's team? I guess I saw that coming. I hope you get better soon, I mean, without rushing of course, and that your son is doing better. Is there anything you need?"

I missed the sense of self-worth I'd had when I was working. I could hear the sense of purpose in Emma's voice. She was in a driven world, a game with rules and roles and triumphs and setbacks and I was unable to feel that belonging anymore.

Over time, I came to understand that I was avoiding boredom in order to hide from my fears. If I could only stay one step ahead of boredom, I would never have long minutes or hours or months of waiting to know whether my fears would be realized. Years later I am working my way up, working my way out of a bad relationship. I am working my way through my son's chronic illness. I am taking on new roles because I can make that decision; I can conquer the new role, I can bend it to my will and feel my worth.

SALLY

SALLY lives in the UK with her husband, Todd, and their daughter, Gemma. Sally spoke to us five years after experiencing burnout while working as a HR director within the UK public sector. In her role, she had a number of complex stakeholders to manage including her line manager, Clement, and her chairman, George. One of her colleagues was named Jimmy and her PA's name was Lilly.

---

8 FEBRUARY 2017, 9.10 AM

Dear Clement,

I look forward to going through my presentation for the board with you. I understand Jimmy will be there as well, although I don't expect he will present the people side of things as he has not been involved in any of the decisions or planning. We can discuss this when we meet.

Speak soon,
Sally

8 FEBRUARY 2017, 11.30 AM

Dear Sally,

I have asked Jimmy to present to the board instead.
This should free up time for you, which I know you need.
Things have been complicated since you joined and
I look forward to concentrating on strategy with you.

Please forward your presentation to Jimmy.

Thanks,
Clement

---

8 FEBRUARY 2017, 12:15 PM

Dear Clement,

I have to say, I don't understand. We agreed that the
relationship with the board is crucial to my success
in this role. Could we please discuss the decision to
have Jimmy replace me in the meeting?

Sally

9 FEBRUARY 2017, 8.02 AM

Dear Gemma,

Thanks for calling last night. I apologize for being so low in energy. I have to admit this new boss is really getting under my skin. I don't trust his decisions. I don't really trust anything he says to me. He seems to want to punish me for doing a good job. Being outspoken has always helped in the past, but with Clement it backfires every time. I feel he is chipping away at me.

Anyway darling, I will be OK, just wanted to explain my fatigue. Looking forward to seeing you in a few weeks on your holiday.

Love,
Mum

---

15 FEBRUARY 2017, 9.37 AM

Lilly (via WhatsApp): Clement just called and made me go through all your appointments this week. I'm so sorry. He literally made me do it. I'm so sorry.

Sally: Don't worry Lilly. I am sorry he put you in this position. I will speak to him.

Lilly: He threatened me about it if I didn't do it.

Sally: He should not have done that. But there is nothing to worry about. I will handle him.

Lilly: Please be careful. I don't trust him.

Sally: Thanks.

15 FEBRUARY 2017, 10.35 AM

Dear Clement,

When we meet, I would like to discuss why you found it necessary to go through my agenda with Lilly earlier this morning. She felt very uncomfortable and did not want to betray my trust, as we have a wonderful working relationship. I also feel uncomfortable, as I would have gladly moved things around if you had asked me.

I will see you at 18:00.

Sally

16 FEBRUARY 2017, 11.12 AM

Dear George,

I am reaching out because I have reached an impasse with Clement. Today he forced Lilly to walk him through all the appointments I had this week and cancelled some of my meetings so that he could schedule a performance review with me. He then sat me down in his office and made it clear that I do not have the right to contest this action of his, that my working time belongs to him and he is free to summon me at any time. He threatened me with taking away my exposure to the board as well as the decision-making power I have to hire and fire personnel at all levels. I find this unethical and a clear instance of bullying. This was not the agreement when I took the job as Head of People. I am clearly mandated to make decisions and act on them and his remit is to support and guide me in those, not to take full control. George, I am not asking for any action on your part, I simply feel I need to log this incident with you as my superior, as it definitely feels I am on shaky ground with Clement. I don't believe this is due to the work I am doing, as my performance speaks for itself, but due to Clement's and my inter-personal dynamic. I am doing my best to work through this, but it seems at this point that his only purpose is to control me and take away any independence or decisions I may have.

Thank you as always for your support,

Sally

16 FEBRUARY 2017, 2.23 PM

Dear Sally,

Thank you for bringing this to my attention. I am so sorry this has taken a rough turn. I can only imagine how terrible this must feel. Please know how much I and the rest of the board appreciate your work. Let me know if there is anything in particular I can do to help you. As this is confidential between us there is little that I can act on, but I am here to support you as needed.

Best,
George

---

23 FEBRUARY 2017, 7:03 PM

Hi Dad,

Just talked to Mum. She had forgotten that I was coming tomorrow for the weekend and needed to leave Fifi with you. Is she OK? She seemed confused and not able to handle walking Fifi twice a day. I know you'll be there too, but she was scaring me. Seemed kinda disoriented. I can talk after 4.

Gemma

1 MARCH 2017

Dear Dr Shores,

As I shared with you confidentially, I cannot go off sick for any psychological or emotional reasons, as I am certain that Clement will use this against me. His tone when I spoke to him yesterday was the same as in that horrible meeting we had: his voice in a sickly sweet tone, as if he was soothing a small child, but overacting the part. He seemed crazy. Psychopathic. It is still giving me chills when I think about it.

Thank you for keeping this between us and for offering to sign me off sick for a gynaecological issue. I don't want to lie but it's important that people not question this, and this feels like a good safeguard. You asked me to briefly describe how I feel: the main things seem to be memory and focus. I am forgetting whole parts of conversations and ensuing tasks. People remind me of things I have said and I can't recall. I am having trouble getting things done when I am usually very task focused. I realize that I am not making progress and it just makes me break down in tears. I used to be so confident and courageous, but I feel scared and threatened all the time. I am doing my best to hand things over today and tomorrow and will then go on full rest beginning this weekend, as you know. I hope we can continue to check in weekly.

Gratefully,
Sally

23 MARCH 2018

Hi darling,

I do hope your travel is going well. As the time difference prevents us from talking much, I thought I would write. You were right when you heard in my voice that I am stumbling again. I feel myself weakening, my courage waning again, not as acutely as when I was working for Clement, but in this new job I need to muster so much energy just to be myself. Maybe I didn't wait long enough. Maybe I need more time to recover. But it's been over a year now and still I blow over in the smallest gust. I don't think this position is going to work out. I feel my boundaries are threatened all the time and I am not sure whether that is real, or whether I need to be clear for myself what my boundaries are. The hierarchy again presses down on me here. HR is the bottom of the food chain and as a woman I feel doubly silenced as HR and as the only female in the room most of the time. These guys are polite, but they still expect me to comply even against my better judgement. With Clement it was directly about control and power and his sick obsession with making me bow down to his authority. He wanted to punish me for standing up to him. Now it is more about me, my style, where and how I fit, my choices. This place is more subtly patriarchal but it is asking me to decide what kind of structure I can be in and be true to myself. I wish I could turn off my heart some days. Hibernate. You don't need to worry because I am taking care of myself. This email is proof of that. And I won't be hasty, but by the end of the year I would like to step out again, maybe work for myself. I hope this does not come as a shock or a worry. I am here when you wake up if you have time to talk, though we can also wait until you are home.

Have a great day ahead, my sweet.

All my love,
Mum

Hi Mum,

Thanks for coming to my concert last night. It was so good to see you shiny and bright and energetic. I see you caring for yourself and the difference that is making. I was struck by what you said about the road to burnout being long and that for a long time you didn't realize it was happening, but it already was. I wonder how many people I know here at university are on that road already. There is so much competition. I feel oddly far from that, maybe because I have seen you learn to be hypervigilant about going too far, about taking care of your self-esteem and your rest. I think that helps me too.

Love you Mum,
Gemma

DOMINIC

DOM is a New Yorker who now lives in Switzerland. He worked in the City of London for 20 years as a hedge fund trader, but had left the industry five years prior to our interview following his experience of burnout. His story is related from the point of view of one of his friends.

When Dom started his work in the City, he retained his buoyant gait and banter much longer than any of us expected. His smile was an open doorway to good times, late nights, weekend plans to discover new and curious corners of the world. We all tagged along with the ease of being led through the streets from place to place, talking and laughing and walking arm in arm without having to know the way. We were advancing together, elbows linked, through our bubbling youth. His baritone voice filled our ears like liquid, spreading through every corner – not loud, but rich and full of promise. I remained single, as he did throughout that time, and we laughed and traded knowing looks as we watched others pair off, branch out, double up, drop off. His first boss treated him well. He felt seen and heard. He was taken in under a wing that was flying but also nurturing. I saw the trust the boss placed in him, whatever his name was – he was there for Dom and this made him believe despite the other tales. Dom once told me his boss believed in the magic of Christmas long after his friends did because he had no first-hand evidence that Santa Claus was a hoax and commercial ploy.

I remember when that boss left for greener pastures, Dom began to see the trickery in the system, the guys getting rewarded with pots of gold while others did the work. He did the work often and was told, for one reason or another, "Not this time, buddy. Don't worry, your moment will come. Keep it up." And so he did. It was just one bad boss, he said to me. And then there was another. The recognition was there within reach, but you had to step on heads to get your fingers around it. "It's a game," he told me, "and you have to tick all these boxes even though doing good work is often something other than the boxes to tick. I just have to hang in there a little longer, stay in the game, until I get rewarded for all this work."

The game dragged on and Dom was weary. He tried to date people, even when he couldn't find the energy. "Fridays I am too shattered," he admitted. "How can I switch from 24/7 numbers and decisions and calls and mistakes and emails and people yelling at each other and two hours later, after a quick shower, be ready to ask some nice woman about her life and really listen? I find it hard to care." So Saturday nights were sacred. The one night in the week when he could get himself to look into a date's eyes, to fantasize for a moment about having time for weekends away and boat trips and walks and meeting her family. Short-lived fantasy. Sunday brought brunch and the gym and making sure his blue and white shirts were prepared for the week. The knot in his stomach, which fully subsided and loosened its grip for a brief moment on Saturdays, slowly took hold of him as he ramped up for the battle ahead.

There was one boss early in the investment phase who had promised him a partnership, a crazy upside, a wild ride, his ship coming in. Come Christmas he was saying, "This was not your year, buddy, but give it time." Dom brooded for a month but got back on the horse. Of course, the boss, father of three and then four, made his share. After all, he was the boss and had a family to look after. "You'll get yours," he said with a thump on the shoulder, "Gotta pay your dues." After three years of "not quite" Dom changed firms again, chasing the promise and adrenaline of a new horizon. He was a hard worker and he cared and he had this sense that he would eventually find fair payback for his earnest efforts.

Then there was the boss who had a substance issue. Alcohol always, and increasingly drugs. He would often miss whole mornings because he couldn't get out of bed. "Indisposed," Dom called it. Dom kept it to himself, except for telling me on our occasional Friday night walks. He had to make decisions while the boss man slept it off. If the decisions were successful, the boss had "taught him well." If not, Dom hadn't listened, hadn't learned, needed more grooming. He gave up dating altogether during this time, besides a forced double date here and there. His arms looked heavy as he lifted his pint and his smile was slower to bloom, like he was in a slow-motion bubble as I walked into the pub to meet him. "I'm OK," he said to me, "but I haven't really slept in weeks. It all gets in my head and the worry and the decisions and being left alone to manage keep me in this state of high alert." And then one day, arms looking leaden, he told me he had quit. He was eerily silent after he told me. There didn't seem to be anything to add. "I just quit. I've had enough. I don't believe. I am free."

And yet he did not seem free for some time. First he disappeared. No dates, no pints, no weekend outings. Then he started to travel: Australia, California, Spain, Florida. He followed his love of tennis and theatre. When I saw him do improv for the first time, his lightness flooded over me and reminded me of the friend I had once had. He kept coming back, more frequently, more naturally, shining through the disappointment. He became excited again at the thought of Wimbledon, Thai food, walking in London and visiting friends. I was glad he had come back.

He called on a Saturday evening: "I got paid for my first gig! This thousand pounds feels so much more real than all those hundreds of thousands that didn't feel like enough. I did something real," he beamed. "I'm real."

ANANYA

ANANYA is a health and wellbeing coach. She grew up in Australia but had lived and worked in Spain for the past ten years at the time we spoke to her. When we met, she had just been signed off work for three weeks due to burnout. She lives with her husband, Mark, and her stepson, Oliver.

Birthday messages were flooding in as if riding the sunlight streaming in the window. It was Saturday, so I had allowed myself to take my tea back to bed while Mark got Oliver out of the door to his basketball practice. "Enjoy the day. Best birthday wishes. Treat yourself. To many more. Younger every year. You rock. Best birthday to my best friend. Love and kisses for a great birthday ..." and on like that for minutes of scrolling. Do I respond to each one? Should I post a blanket thanks? I heard the door slam as Mark and Oliver headed out. The blank bedroom walls were as silent as the wall of messages. I struggled to hear their sound, to imagine the voices, their tone, the warmth, the music. Next year I would turn 50.

I didn't feel almost 50. God knows I might not have made it this far. A heart attack at 38 had made me a medical anomaly and a walking poster child for healthy living. I was now a certified health coach and a yoga teacher who loved hot chocolate – real hot chocolate, preferably Belgian with whipped cream and raw cocoa sprinkled over it – almost as much as the searing sun of the Australian back garden where I spent most of my childhood hours drawing the flowers my father grew.

What had I done in this half century? I pondered as my eyes shifted from the messages on my phone to the yellow walls around me. Had I become the woman I wanted to be? Was I whole, was I healthy, was I sane? What was my impact on the world around me and what was in my hands to change? As I interrogated myself, I felt the child in me turning to draw flowers instead of joining the debate team as my father had wished. There is a strange counter-movement in folding inwards to catch on paper the open reach of an orange tiger lily.

I didn't draw a flower. I started the 365-day count-down to my 50th birthday. I resolved to become that woman I aspired to be. I gave up sugar (even my beloved hot chocolate), gluten, alcohol, gossip and laziness. I painted the bedroom a cool green and rearranged my office to reflect a clean and composed inner state. I focused on betterment of myself, my surroundings and even my loved ones. I wanted to be a better step-mom, a better wife, a better daughter – despite the half a world of distance between me and my parents in Australia and the blossoming pandemic, which would keep me in these newly painted walls for most of the hours and minutes until the momentous five-oh.

The piece I could not seem to wedge neatly into the betterment puzzle was my job: I had once loved my work, but since my employer had been bought by a larger firm, I had felt completely valueless in my role. My boss had left and my new boss had spoken with me twice in a year. My efforts seemed to feed a beast I had never seen but that took on strange forms in my imagination, sometimes animal, sometimes machine, never human. We had an arrangement though, me and the beast. I would work tirelessly, striving to be recognized and rewarded in this new system, and the beast would hang a carrot (or a hot chocolate) just close enough that it seemed within reach as long as I pedalled just a tiny bit faster. But I could never seem to catch it. Always just out of my grasp was the feeling of being included, appreciated, valued for what I did. I needed to strive a bit harder to get there. I could feel myself flagging. Week by week, a gradual waning of my energy. Just a slightly harder push, I told myself, and I would break through. But every 'one last push' required a bit more heat, as if my engine needed a hotter and hotter spark to ignite.

Mark complained that I was absent. Oliver quipped, "You're losing your grip," when I accidentally drove him to school instead of basketball. I knew I was tired, but I held on with the determination of a child playing tug of war. I thought I could win. A few weeks after turning 50 (the party Mark threw for me had been lovely and a blur), I took a planned week off work. I was feeling the exhaustion creeping in and a week away, even if just a two-hour drive from home, would give me the chance to slow down, stare at the lake from the hotel porch, have meals out, with Mark and Oliver enjoying tennis while I read and took long walks. Mark noted how much I was sleeping. I wondered whether animals in hibernation notice that change or whether it is so engrained in them that they adjust unconsciously. I would not have noticed without Mark's help.

We returned home on a Saturday evening after a misty drive over soft grassy hills. On Sunday afternoon I decided I had better turn on my computer before post-holiday Monday hit me. I sat down in the armchair in the corner of my small yellow office and opened my email app. Updating folders: bold blue subject lines started to populate the screen, randomly filling the screen from above and below as messages loaded and the app put them in chronological order. It was like watching a waterfall, with splashes jumping

here and there. My hands felt heavy and numb holding the edges of my laptop and I watched the keyboard getting splashed with drops. For a moment I
didn't know where they were coming from. I was as
helpless to stop the flow of tears as I was the influx of
emails. The words blurred, and I had no sense of their
content or meaning any more than the cause of my
crying. They flooded forth together. I found myself
on the floor, still crying, the woolly carpet itching my
wet cheek. "I can't, I just can't," I said to Mark when
he found me. He gave up asking questions and helped
me to bed.

I didn't want to tell anyone at work. I was scared. I
didn't want to lose my job. I didn't want to say I wasn't
coping. When I did contact HR after three days of
being off sick, the HR-designated therapist required
that I take another two full weeks off. Warm lines
making their way down my cheeks again. My tears
were like a leak coming from nowhere.

It's been three months now since I was drowning
in a waterfall of emails. I have found joy in cups of
hot chocolate; I have watched myself be intentional
about getting up from my chair and greeting Oliver
when he comes in the door after school. I sit with
him while he makes himself a snack. Sometimes we
talk, sometimes he hums to himself. I am here to
witness him. Our evenings start earlier and end later.
Mark is attentive, as if I were a delicate plant that
needed careful pruning. He is still wary of words, so
a lot goes unsaid, or said to friends instead of Mark,
but I feel cared for. I feel, again. I am trying to stop.

Stop chasing empty goals. Stop attending meetings that are about things far from my heart: new platforms, new wellbeing tools to sell clients, new packaging of old things. I am starting to work four days a week and trying to make the hours and days count by working on things I care about. I weigh whether there is a compelling reason for many of the calls I join, of which there are fewer, by design. Every rejected meeting is a victory.

I have started meeting neighbours. We have a group of theatre-goers. We keep in touch by WhatsApp, proposing plays and outings. We go out for drinks or dinner. I still need lots of sleep and growing amounts of hot chocolate. I often type emails sitting in my armchair instead of leaning forward at my desk. I fall asleep sometimes, hands on the keyboard, head fallen back on the backrest of the chair, mouth open, ears oblivious, time gone. I become conscious that I am asleep and will myself to close my mouth or wiggle my toes, but the slumber keeps its hold. Eventually I find a wilful path to consciousness, like pushing through thick liquid. I surrender to these moments. I bow to the fickle goddess of fatigue. Rain and rest are my refuge.

MALCOLM

When **MALCOLM** experienced burnout, he was working as head of learning and development for a family-owned multinational in Asia. At around the same time, Malcolm's wife, a senior manager in logistics, was also experiencing burnout. Malcolm is Swedish and lives with his wife and family in Singapore. His story is told from the point of view of his boss.

Malcolm was working for me when he broke. I still don't really get it. He was a machine, you know, in a good way. Anything that came his way he would tackle full on and obtain incredible results. One time he had two board members, me as his boss and our events agency all demanding different approaches to the leadership summit he was organizing and he managed to cater to all our needs. I loved it, because even though I fully disagreed with one of the board members, I felt I got what I needed and I never even had to have a conversation with that guy. Malcolm saved me from that confrontation. He probably doesn't even know that to this day, but I am way better off for it.

It's such a shame that he lost the thread of what he was so good at. He worked tirelessly.

I guess there were some signs, like one day he yelled at one of his team members when there were other people, including me, within earshot. I mean, I do that sometimes – we have an assertive culture here – but it was unlike Malcolm. That same week I heard he lost his cool with a manager too at a hotel we'd hired for a summit. He was really stressed about the noise and construction going on during the CEO's speech. We were supposed to record the speech and then use it in a company-wide comms campaign. I guess there was something about how they couldn't edit out background noise and the CEO's office had made it clear that the conditions needed to be absolutely perfect or they would not allow the video to be used. I think Malcolm stayed up several nights in a row leading up to the event. I told him, "Buddy, you should get some rest," but I knew he wouldn't let anything drop for the sake of a few hours of sleep. And I was confident that in his hands everything would go smoothly. I mean, there wasn't much the rest of us could do to help. He had it all in his head, and his team was good. And this was his jam. He was proud of having been appointed as the leader of the summit and it was a high-stakes gig. He knew he had a lot to gain. I have no idea how he managed with his family and everything. I heard his wife had a burnout too, about a year after he did. I know they were both working, they had two kids and they had just moved to a new house. His career was on the rise, but he couldn't have had much time for himself or his family. Maybe that's what got him, although I know plenty of people here who have gone through a period like that for a couple of years or even more. I would say it tends to pay off. It's hard for me to say, since I was hired in at the exec level and never had to work up through the ranks here. At my previous company, it was different.

It was a two-hour drive home from the summit. Everything had gone perfectly. The CEO's office was really happy and congratulated me. Malcolm seemed happy too, although he was quiet. He looked like he was forcing himself to smile when the MC thanked him and his team at the end. He was driving the van because it was rented in his name and at one point I looked over and saw that he was crying while he was driving. I thought maybe the late afternoon sun was bothering him, but he didn't say anything and I didn't want to make it worse. I guess all the tension must have got to him. After we stopped for a break, one of his team members took over the driving and he seemed OK. It was the following week that he finally hit a wall and couldn't come to work. Our business partner called me to say he was on medical leave and would be out for two weeks. Two weeks! That was like a whole summer holiday. I didn't think it would take him that long to rest up and there was plenty of follow-up to be done from the summit, but he really did disappear. They took him to a special clinic and I hear he slept for most of the two weeks. He wasn't even allowed to check his email and stay in touch. I thought it must have been driving him crazy to be so cut off after being the nerve centre for the whole thing, but apparently he needed it.

He came back part time and seemed himself except he was more subdued. I remember noticing that when we received a query about launching a new leadership framework, he asked a lot of questions about how it was going to be put in place and what the goals would be instead of saying, "Yes, leave it with me, we will make this happen," like he would have done before. The CEO's deputy came and asked me about it. Why were we questioning things instead of delivering? Was Malcolm the right guy for the job? Luckily right at that time he was up for a promotion, which meant he was no longer the front man for the events or the framework. I was leaving to go to a role in Beijing, so I basically lost track of Malcolm – as his boss, I mean. He had a global role, so I still had contact with him. But when he relapsed, I was not aware of it until months later. I heard he had to step away again, this time for several months because he couldn't cope with work. Then at the end of that medical leave, he decided not to return. I heard from someone on his team that he had become increasingly tired, unable to work the hours that it took to deliver the job. It's amazing when I think about what he was capable of before. He was a star and really cared about the outcome. People liked him too. Now there are two people doing that job essentially.

If I'm honest, I need people like Malcolm on my team – people who really care and are able to push things to a new level. I need to oversee things and manage the politics, but the people on the ground, like Malcolm, have to be able to work at two levels. They need the intellectual power of a top leader and the drive of a front-line worker. I think Malcolm's drive was too strong in the end. He was effective while it lasted, but he pushed himself too far.

CHAPTER 6

WHAT HAVE WE LEARNED?

"IF BURNOUT PERVADES IN AN ORGANIZATION, IT'S TELLING YOU THERE'S A TOXIC ENVIRONMENT HERE, THAT IT'S NOT A HEALTHY PLACE TO BE."[56]

CHRISTINA MASLACH, 2021

Our desire to share stories is part of what makes us human,[57] and being able to talk about our struggles in conversation with others can help us to make sense of our experiences.[58] We are deeply grateful to all those who told their stories of burnout, of which there are many more than the five we were able to feature in *Chapter 5*. In this chapter, we offer an interpretation of the themes that we saw emerging across these five songs of burnout. We appreciate that there are many ways to tell and to interpret a story.[59] Therefore, we imagine that you as readers may also bring your own interpretations to bear, particularly in relation to the elements of the stories that resonate with your own experience.

In *Chapter 2*, we suggested that burnout continues because of the nature of workplaces today,[60] be it the intense demands that are placed upon us, having to work with inadequate resources, or the disconnect between our employer's espoused values and our day-to-day experiences of those values enacted at work. Burnout occurs when there is a mismatch between expectation and reality. Research has shown that this mismatch tends to occur across six domains: workload, control, reward, community, fairness and values.[61] When it comes to Chelsea, Sally, Dom, Ananya and Malcolm, we see all of these domains playing out in different ways. However, their experiences of burnout are nuanced, such that we cannot simply pinpoint an unmanageable workload, a lack of autonomy, not being fairly rewarded, interpersonal conflict, unfair treatment or a values mismatch as *the* single trigger. Instead, these stories demonstrate the complex interplay between an individual's personality, their work context and the circumstances going on in their personal lives at the time that lead to the perfect storm.

In all of the stories, there was a point at which wanting to do a good job became bad for the person's health. We know that work can bring us a sense of self-worth and a sense of belonging.[62] However, studies have also shown that we can have too much of a good thing when it comes to our relationship with work. Overidentification with our job is both a "social cure" and a "motivational primer" for us to work harder.[63] Identifying with a particular group or team at work can satisfy our innate desire for belonging, bringing us much-needed social connection and support. At the same time, a strong sense of belonging can act as a primer to push us to work harder, take on more responsibilities and help colleagues even if not formally requested to do so.[64] It is our motivational drivers, such as our need to feel valued and our need for social bonds, that become the very things that can lead to overwork, even workaholism.[65] Those people who tend to overidentify with their jobs, such as Chelsea and Malcolm, are those whose sense of self-worth is irrevocably tied up with work. Overcommitted employees have been described as having "difficulty withdrawing from work – continuously striving for high achievement because of an extreme need for approval and esteem from work."[66]

Studies have also shown that there are personality traits that may be more prone to workaholism and burnout than others, such as perfectionism. In work contexts where long hours are the norm and maintaining safety and high standards is critical (such as law, medicine and aviation), highly conscientious individuals have been found to be more vulnerable to burnout.[67] It may be the mix of contextual factors and individual traits that provides the rocket fuel for burnout. Individuals with certain dispositions – such as those with high standards for themselves and worries about making mistakes in front of others (the two elements of perfectionism)[68] – can experience workaholism when they find themselves in the wrong kind of environment, and workaholism in turn has been found to lead to exhaustion, a central quality of burnout.[69] This is perhaps unsurprising when we consider that workaholics do not get enough sleep, exercise or leisure time. Furthermore, workaholics have been found to have lower levels of happiness with life outside work, which perhaps further compounds their need to work in pursuit of fulfilment.[70] It appears that in Malcolm's case in particular, he became so consumed by work demands and the desire to do a good job that he found himself sacrificing his own health to the point of exhaustion in service of the organization.

In Chelsea's story, the physical, mental and emotional impacts of overidentification with work are clear. We know that in challenging situations, the brain initiates a hormonal (endocrine) response, where glucocorticoids, including cortisol, are released. Research has shown that prolonged stress can impair hormone function, leading to problems including immune disorders.[71] In Chelsea's case, the story was in her blood, which was showing a decimated white cell count and several impaired hormone functions. Chelsea may have been working herself to death, as we know that chronic stress has a potentially catastrophic impact on our health, increasing our risk of heart disease by up to 40% as well as increasing our susceptibility to strokes and high blood pressure.[72] When it comes to the impact of burnout on memory in particular, some studies suggest a link between reduced cognitive function and burnout,[73] which in Chelsea's case manifested as amnesia. Given the intensity of the demands in her work and home life, it became easier for Chelsea to shut down than to experience so many difficult emotions at once. Chelsea's experience of numbness is not unique in the 'always on' culture experienced by many working professionals. Given the constant demands for workers to demonstrate their productivity and performance, "numbness is a way to cope."[74] The stress Chelsea was experiencing became so overwhelming that her brain appeared to use dissociation as a defence mechanism to cope.[75] Research also suggests that burnout can affect concentration and memory lapses in everyday tasks,[76] which seems to have been the case both for Sally and Chelsea.

Despite certain personality traits being more vulnerable to burnout than others, when it comes to the relational aspects of our work, it is the bond we have with our line manager that can make or break our sense of engagement and wellbeing.[77] Research suggests that line managers carry a disproportionate influence when it comes to burnout – either preventing or promoting burnout depending on the extent to which their leadership has a constructive or destructive impact. Positive leadership behaviours that have been found to help prevent burnout include support (e.g. emotional support offered with empathy and compassion and practical support in the form of access to resources, information and advice); quality of relationships (i.e. the extent to which reporting relationships are based on mutual trust and respect); and influence (e.g. being an empowering coach and positive role model).[78] On the other hand, destructive leadership behaviours that have been found to promote burnout include bullying, verbal and non-verbal aggression, blaming others, breaking promises and expressing anger.[79] These harmful methods of influence are shockingly clear in Sally's case in her manager's attempts to scare her into submission through bullying, control and insidious emotional gaslighting. Nobody should have to suffer at the hands of an abusive boss; however, research suggests that three in every ten leaders display toxic behaviours.[80]

Moreover, it is not just overtly negative behaviours that drain energy, cause stress and contribute to burnout; studies show that "passive-avoidant" leadership can be equally destructive.[81] These behaviours include turning a blind eye to dysfunctional or damaging behaviours in organizations, regularly being unavailable or absent, and avoiding difficult conversations.[82] In Sally's case, it appears that the chairman's inaction following the concerns she raised about her manager's toxic behaviour was a form of passive-avoidant leadership, which further contributed to her alienation from work. Both Dominic and Malcolm also appeared to experience aspects of laissez-faire leadership: Dominic had to cover for a regularly absent boss and Malcolm's line manager was complicit with and encouraging of a culture of overwork. Malcolm's, Sally's and Dominic's organizational environments appeared to be quagmires of toxicity. A toxic work culture:

"Erodes, disables and destroys the physiological, psychosocial and spiritual wellbeing of the people who work in it in permanent and deliberate ways. In other words, an organization becomes metaphorically a 'poison pill' for employees."[83]

There were several women among our research co-contributors. Looking at Chelsea's, Sally's and Ananya's stories in particular, we can see that experiences of burnout are not gender neutral. We know that women and men do not share the same experiences of work, with many women continuing to battle for equal opportunities and equal pay; for women of colour, immigrant women and women with children, these challenges are even greater.[84] Research suggests that female professionals are exposed to more stress at work than their male counterparts, because they are more likely to face harassment, sex discrimination, gender stereotyping and a lack of organizational support when trying to combine their career with family care responsibilities.[85] The COVID-19 pandemic presented another level of challenge to them as women. As the pandemic took hold and the world went into lockdown, they found themselves also being primarily responsible for childcare, while shouldering the brunt of domestic chores at the same time as they were trying to hold down demanding full-time jobs. For some men, home might feel like a place of rest and recuperation from work; however, for many women especially during the pandemic, home became a site of additional unpaid work – a "second shift," as some put it.[86] One study suggests that working women with children were at increased risk of burnout during the pandemic, particularly when the boundaries between home and work became blurred.[87]

We know from their stories that some of our co-contributors felt that their unhealthy work cultures were too entrenched to change, particularly Sally, Dominic and Malcolm. They each ended up taking the decision to quit their jobs and leave their organization, believing that in the end, the need for self-preservation trumped any desire to drive for systemic change.

It is all too easy for employers to try to 'fix' overwhelmed and overworked employees with a week off work or wellbeing initiatives.[88] In all five songs of burnout, we can see that time off work gave the individuals some temporary respite, yet the root causes of burnout remained. To truly tackle burnout, not only do we need to challenge societal norms and expectations concerning work as *the* source of our fulfilment in life, but we also need to pay attention to the organizational environments we find ourselves caught up in. Like Dominic, we can become seduced by the promise of a pot of gold at the end of the rainbow; like Chelsea, we may find ourselves unable to detach because our sense of self is so tightly bound to the role we play; or like Malcolm, it might be the distinctive character strengths that initially serve us well that in the end become our Achilles heel.[89] From the stories we have heard, it is those people who act with tough compassion who are the ones who are able to save their souls. Tough compassion means being able to spot and surface our own (and others') unhealthy behaviours before it is too late.[90] It means facing up to difficult conversations about the detrimental impact of work cultures, and it means living with clearer boundaries between work and non-work in service of our long-term wellbeing. That said, tough compassion can take its toll when attempts at dialogue are dismissed or blocked. However, in the end, the decision to leave an organization is sometimes the most compassionate thing we can do for ourselves. As Elizabeth Svoboda writes, "Exiting from a harmful situation can be its own form of uncompromising truth-telling."[91]

At the end of the interviews with our co-contributors, we asked each of them how it felt to tell us their stories. It was the first time some of them had disclosed their experiences to anyone beyond their immediate family, whereas others had talked (or were talking) about their experiences within therapy settings. Despite their different paths to burnout, one theme united all their experiences: despite the passage of time, there was much that remained unresolved about their experiences of burnout. Whether their burnout was current or had been experienced in the past, no one felt they had fully recovered. Several of them even questioned whether recovery from burnout was ever possible. Instead, they said they were learning how to live in its shadow and accept that they must constantly negotiate its boundaries. When it comes to their relationship with work, they said that it was an ongoing struggle to find a 'Goldilocks point' where work's hold over them was neither too much, pulling them back into burnout, nor too little, meaning that they lost their much-needed sense of purpose, direction and progress.

Like water finding its way to the sea through and around any obstacle, the people who told us their stories all shared an irrepressible desire to prevail. They had all been profoundly changed by the experience of burnout, but most had found their way back to a balance that was more attuned to their needs and to the dangers that lie in excessive work. Many of them referred to knowing their limits better, communicating what they would and would not do, and shaping the work conditions they needed to attempt to remain whole. The people we spoke to, both in the gathering of individual stories and in the community inquiry conversations, described practices that had helped them to heal and to remain healthy and self-aware in the face of demanding, high-pressure or intensely emotional work. These healing practices are the focus of the next chapter.

CHAPTER 7

FINDING OUR WAY BACK

"YOUR BODY HAS THINGS TO SAY."

I SAID BACK TO MYSELF,

"I WILL TRY AND LISTEN"[92]

BESSEL VAN DER KOLK, 2014

Both of us, along with our co-contributors, have been able to nurture our own wellbeing through a range of activities that, because they have brought us solace, we have adopted as personal customs to enhance our way of being in relation to our work. In my case (Katherine), I started doing yoga some years ago because I was depressed and confused and the demands on me both at work and at home seemed insurmountable. The physical awareness, movement and breathing that a 15- to 20-minute morning yoga habit afforded me did not solve my dilemmas directly, but they seemed to give me the space to get through yet another confounding day without breaking. I came to trust that, though I did not know exactly how the yoga sequence was helping, I was evolving through this new habit in ways that felt connected to purpose, quality and self-care. In both of our experience, then, an activity becomes a practice when you trust it enough to engage with it on a long-term basis with intention and curiosity. I find that when I return to my mat after many days of travel and other interruptions, I am able to meet myself there with gratitude and renewed commitment to keep listening to my body even when the din of daily life makes it hard to hear.

In conducting this research, we have begun to understand the ways in which individuals protect themselves in the face of burnout, in post-burnout or in guarding against burnout. Strikingly, all of these methods are embodied, meaning that our bodies and our physical existence are central features in these approaches. From the stillness of meditation to the explosiveness of running or kickboxing, or the mindful physicality of painting and photography, the sustaining practices we have gathered all share an embodied quality.

As Carol Dweck advocates in her famous work on the virtues of adopting a growth mindset, we are all a work in progress – one that evolves, changes, grows and learns from failure and setbacks.[110] In many ways the idea of resilience, which means finding our way back to our original shape, somewhat misses the important aspect of learning, growing and changing through our experiences. The members of our research groups reinforced the idea that post-burnout, they had become new versions of themselves, ones that had learned some important limits and incorporated one or more of the practices described in this chapter. We know from our experience and theirs that finding and honing your own practices by listening to your whole being and adjusting whenever the need arises is a highly personal endeavour.

something that started long before he started crying during the journey home after his company's big event. None of them were aware of their eroding sense of self, health, balance or personal sustainability until it was too late. Essentially, they ploughed on for months (and in some cases years) in a state of mind–body dislocation, which is the antithesis of mindfulness.

While meditation and mindfulness at first glance may seem to happen in the mind (and 'mindfulness' even contains the word itself), the awareness created in all the practices we have collected through our research is in direct relation to the body. Meditation practices focus initially on the breath, inviting us to notice the bodily phenomenon of breathing in and out and doing so consciously, with full awareness. Mindfulness, or being aware of our own state as we move through the various moments of our lives, invites connection between body, mind, emotion, intention and spirit.

MOVEMENT

Exercise and movement are known to be classic de-stressors. How many of us rely on getting out for a run, a walk, a game of tennis or a dance class to wash away the trials and tribulations of work and even to act as a buffer between work and home life? For Amy, daily swims have become her movement of choice. During the height of the pandemic when gyms and leisure centres were closed, she turned to local lakes and rivers. Being immersed in water, hearing herself breathe and feeling the regular rhythm of her stroke became her metronome, helping to clear her mind from work, renew her body and enliven her soul. Igor found exercise to be effective during the first phase of the COVID-19 pandemic, helping him to get in shape and bringing the immediate benefit of the endorphins that result from a good run. Exercise of many kinds reminds us that we have a body and that we are giving ourselves the time and permission to practise self-care. Because enjoyable exercise can look vastly different from one individual to another, it is important to find an exercise practice that suits us to avoid it becoming one more chore to add to the to-do list, something that will eventually stress us further because we feel obliged to do it.

THE BODY AS A SOURCE OF KNOWLEDGE AND HEALING

It can seem paradoxical that the antidote to a mental illness, breakdown or setback is best accessed through the body and not directly through the mind. When Bessel van der Kolk began practising psychology as a recent graduate of Harvard Medical School in the early 1970s, drug treatment for patients with Post-traumatic Stress Disorder (PTSD) was all the rage. New pharmacological treatments were being discovered and used abundantly. But van der Kolk began to question such practices and was inclined to use talk therapy to get to know what was going on for his patients, what triggered their flashbacks and fear, and how memories and associations could take them right back to the events that had caused their trauma. Many traumatized patients, however, were not able to jump directly into talking and expressing their experiences and feelings, or even writing about them. In his book *The Body Keeps the Score*, van der Kolk recounts his journey into discovering not only how our bodies house our experiences and our trauma, often blocking certain physical abilities or even making us ill or injured, but also how they can be a gateway to accessing, expressing and relieving the effects of trauma:

"One of the clearest lessons from contemporary neuroscience is that our sense of ourselves is anchored in a vital connection with our bodies. We do not truly know ourselves unless we can feel and interpret our physical sensations. We need to register and act on these sensations to navigate safely through life."[93]

We have made the link in previous chapters between burnout and trauma. However, we do not need to experience trauma, or know whether our experiences with overwork constitute trauma, to be able to benefit from self-knowledge, healing and prevention through the body. Some of the practices that we describe here were brought to our attention by our inquiry participants and some we have discovered ourselves as we have navigated tendencies toward overwork and exhaustion.

MEDITATION AND MINDFULNESS

Meditation and mindfulness, while related to each other, are two different practices. We group them together here partly to offer the distinction between them, partly because they both draw on awareness as their main source, and partly because incorporating both into daily practice is a powerful way of sustaining ourselves in the face of burnout.

Meditation is the intentional practice of placing our awareness on something. There are various types of meditation that place awareness on different areas. For example, breath concentration ('mindful breathing' or *anapanasati*) is a tried and tested way of 'building the muscle' of concentration;[94] body scanning is a variant of concentration meditation; kindness meditation is oriented toward self-compassion (and a first step to developing compassion for others);[95] visualizations invite us to picture something in the mind's eye; emotional or relational meditations (*metta*) aim to produce positive emotional states and ways of being with others; and reflection or insight meditations inquire into specific questions, such as "Who am I?" or "Why did this happen to me?" There are many sources on the theory and practice of meditation.

In particular, we have drawn on *Beyond Mindfulness* by Stephan Bodian[96] and *The Science of Enlightenment* by Shinzen Young.[97]

Mindfulness can stem from meditation but does not have to. When we are mindful, we are non-judgementally aware of our mental, physical and emotional state and how this affects our choices, decisions, actions and emotions. We could in fact do everything mindfully and this is often the intent of meditation: to heighten awareness and hence to be more mindful. Indeed, meditation practices also state as an end goal the ability to meditate while going through the activities of our daily lives, though this may feel like a fairly lofty aspiration. We find that the idea of being more mindfully aware of how we are at any given moment feels attainable, and perhaps even essential if we are to protect ourselves from the pressures of intense work and challenging private lives. In fact, many of those who shared their stories of burnout with us had started practising some form of meditation or mindfulness in their efforts to return to wholeness. Most of them had stuck with it, as they realized that slipping into a state of burnout is essentially the opposite of awareness. For example, Chelsea began her story by sharing that her descent into burnout probably started long before the moment when the nurse on her son's ward pointed out that she was abnormally devoid of emotion. Dominic spent his whole banking career chasing the promise of a reward that was never quite close enough to grasp, and Malcolm learned to more clearly detect his tendency toward perfectionism as

something that started long before he started crying during the journey home after his company's big event. None of them were aware of their eroding sense of self, health, balance or personal sustainability until it was too late. Essentially, they ploughed on for months (and in some cases years) in a state of mind–body dislocation, which is the antithesis of mindfulness.

While meditation and mindfulness at first glance may seem to happen in the mind (and 'mindfulness' even contains the word itself), the awareness created in all the practices we have collected through our research is in direct relation to the body. Meditation practices focus initially on the breath, inviting us to notice the bodily phenomenon of breathing in and out and doing so consciously, with full awareness. Mindfulness, or being aware of our own state as we move through the various moments of our lives, invites connection between body, mind, emotion, intention and spirit.

MOVEMENT

Exercise and movement are known to be classic de-stressors. How many of us rely on getting out for a run, a walk, a game of tennis or a dance class to wash away the trials and tribulations of work and even to act as a buffer between work and home life? For Amy, daily swims have become her movement of choice. During the height of the pandemic when gyms and leisure centres were closed, she turned to local lakes and rivers. Being immersed in water, hearing herself breathe and feeling the regular rhythm of her stroke became her metronome, helping to clear her mind from work, renew her body and enliven her soul. Igor found exercise to be effective during the first phase of the COVID-19 pandemic, helping him to get in shape and bringing the immediate benefit of the endorphins that result from a good run. Exercise of many kinds reminds us that we have a body and that we are giving ourselves the time and permission to practise self-care. Because enjoyable exercise can look vastly different from one individual to another, it is important to find an exercise practice that suits us to avoid it becoming one more chore to add to the to-do list, something that will eventually stress us further because we feel obliged to do it.

As humans, we were born to move. In the early 2000s, when I (Katherine) was working in a business school, a colleague and I noticed that over the course of their week-long learning programmes, participants were becoming physically exhausted. So we started to explore what we might be doing to them to inadvertently produce this result. Admittedly, we were submitting them to long days of intellectual and relational challenges in the classroom. But these were generally talented executives on the fast track. Surely they faced more difficult days at work! We were feeding them regularly and they were in a comfortable and safe environment. On closer inspection, however, the physical conditions of the course started to stand out as potentially harmful. The participants were being offered food that was high in simple carbohydrates (such as croissants, sandwiches, fried food, desserts, sugary drinks and alcohol). They were being transported by bus from their hotel to class and back again, with little time at either end of the day for relaxation or exercise. They were being taken out to nice restaurants in the evening for more delicious food and wine. And breakout rooms tended to be as close as possible to the main classroom, thus eliminating almost all incidental movement from the day. On top of all of this, the participants had day jobs and families, both of which tended to keep them up late at night, whether they were checking the work emails they had missed during the day or catching up with their family members. The more they descended into fatigue, the more they felt they needed caffeine and sugar to keep them going. We were essentially sending them on a road to exhaustion by the end of the week. And the programme was supposed to make them better professionals! In 2012 my colleague and I published a paper that documents our findings and the story of reversing this trend by designing physical and mental health into the experience of an executive course.[98]

The benefits of incorporating movement and exercise into our daily lives are well documented. The hormonal changes that occur when we exercise are likely to restore our mind, body and spirit, making this one of the practices that can help us to heal when we have been in or close to burnout. We know from our co-contributors to this book that when we are working too much and too hard, movement and exercise quickly become 'nice-to-haves' and eventually get eliminated from our daily routines. However, those individuals who remain dedicated to getting daily movement and exercise (as long as this remains a release and not one more 'must do') are those who remain connected in body and mind and are able to stave off episodes of burnout. Movement and exercise are perhaps the most common and direct way to keep mind and body connected and healthy, but there are a number of other 'ways in' to this connection, which we will explore in the remainder of this chapter.

SOUND

The most prevalent sound-related wellbeing or healing practice we have come across in our research for this book is making music. Malcolm turned to playing his guitar while in a clinic for six weeks after his worst period of burnout. Others in our community inquiry found solace in dancing or singing, or in making short films set to music from their childhood. Listening to music has been shown to improve our mental wellbeing in several ways. For example, music can improve our mood and motivation, reduce stress, increase relaxation, improve focus, and reduce anxiety and depression.[99] There are also indications that different kinds of music have different effects on our moods: classical, soft and ambient music is best for focus and relaxation, while louder more rhythmic sounds can enliven us and make us want to move. Among our co-contributors, these types of music have proven effective in generating new energy in people who were burnt out.

Also in the aural realm, we spoke to some people who found personal regeneration through walking in the woods and especially listening to the sounds of nature. Studies have pointed to the positive effects of birdsong on our mental health.[100] Bird sounds connect us with nature and to an ancestral feeling of safety due to the presence of birdsong in places where there is water, relative safety from predators, and vegetation providing potential shelter and even nutrition. We will come back to the effects of nature in general on our ability to stave off burnout, but it is clear that the sounds of nature are an important factor in helping us find our way back.

MAKING AND VISUAL ART

When Malcolm was tapping into his love of music and creating it himself, he was experiencing solace related to sound but also related to making music. In the story he shared with us, he also mentioned making music with his daughter, combining sound, creativity and human connection. Another co-inquirer turned to photography as a way of healing from burnout and as a means by which he marked his way back to health. In an entry in his blog, which became part of his practice to return to health, he writes:

"Rather than an intellectual acknowledgement of the insecurities that feed busyness and achievement, I can feel an embodied knowing of how ego is seduced by the status and privilege that overwork promises to provide."[101]

Dominic found energy when he started practising improv theatre and eventually decided to make his new livelihood doing voiceovers. When sharing his story with us, he recounted with visible pride how much he had enjoyed the first time he made money from a voiceover assignment, which was the direct product of his own creativity. His excitement was so much greater than when he had been working in banking despite the remuneration being a fraction of his former earnings. Igor said that a year and a half into the pandemic, feeling deeply overwhelmed and depressed from the repeating and relentless cycles of online work, exercise, sleep, repeat, he found comfort in gardening, especially from the creative perspective of planting, growing and producing something beautiful.

The effects of art on mental health are well documented.[102] One of our own research findings has been that people in burnout become disconnected from their physical selves, and we have found that the physical process of using one's hands to make and create is an important source of positive energy that helps people in the face of burnout and in healing following burnout. Making and visual art offer us a window into what van der Kolk calls "interoception," which is "the ability to be aware of what is going on within us, what we are feeling and even why."[103] When we write some music, photograph something stirring, or paint what we see or imagine, we are taking a step toward interoception. If a central feature of burnout is that we lose much or all of our physical and emotional awareness of ourselves, then artful practices offer a powerful means of helping us find our way back to awareness and self-care.

NATURE

Humans have an innate connection to nature. Nature tends to remind us that we are part of a larger system. Looking up at the stars or watching a spectacular sunset can remind us that perhaps, our trials and tribulations are not as transcendental as they may seem. There is a wealth of research that links contact with nature to increased mental health and wellbeing. Otto Scharmer and Katrin Kaufer's work, for example, highlights the divide between self and nature as one of the major blind spots of our current society.[104] Fritjof Capra's "web of life" describes a holistic view of self, community and planet, offering a mindful approach to being in the world and feeling fully connected that brings together several of the practices described in this chapter.[105]

We and our research participants found time in nature to be soothing, a means of slowing down, and a bringing us new perspectives. The COVID-19 lockdowns were a source of new knowledge about the detriments of not having access to nature, fresh air and sunshine. Chelsea's story vividly describes the healing power of the sun in helping her to reconnect with herself and to find new energy.

THE POWER OF TALKING WITH STRANGERS

As van der Kolk says,

"Telling the story is important. Without stories memory becomes frozen and without memory you cannot imagine how things can be different."[106]

He also noted that "our ability to destroy each other is matched by our ability to restore each other."[107] In his work with trauma patients, van der Kolk highlights the importance of restoring relationships and connection with others as a way of healing. Building on his seminal work, we found that when dealing with the trauma of burnout, it is an important part of the healing practice for individuals to have the ability to forge a new community with people who are not part of their workplace, family or immediate community. Our co-contributors commonly felt hamstrung by social norms and 'feeling rules'[108] about how they should behave at work, coupled with experiencing pressure to perform, and they spoke of the liberating effect of being able to talk to someone they did not know about their struggles. In conversations where there was no shared history and no future, our individual co-contributors felt liberated from expectations to be a certain way or to play a certain role and were therefore more willing to disclose their experiences to someone they did not know because there was no fear of being judged.

What this suggests to us is that in offering support to groups on burnout, organizations and individuals would do well to lean on cross-organizational groups, such as the Running on Empty Rounds that we have established as a result of our research (www.runningonemptyrounds.com), rather than providing in-house forums that would not offer the anonymity of a group of strangers. As Joe Keohane writes,

"Talking to strangers isn't just a way to live. It is a way to survive."[109]

CHAPTER 8

IMAGINING A WAY FORWARD

"WE WILL NOT ERADICATE BURNOUT ALONE."

AMY BRADLEY & KATHERINE SEMLER, 2022

Given its prevalence, we have now reached a point where employers ignore burnout at their peril. We are in the middle of a global mental health crisis, with negative emotions such as worry, stress, anger and sadness reaching record levels. Seven in ten employees now say they are currently struggling or suffering rather than thriving in their lives overall.[111] This widespread societal malaise has led many organizations to focus on employee wellbeing, with initiatives aimed at improving working conditions, such as counselling services, meditation classes and fitness programmes, being launched almost every month. At the height of the pandemic, for example, online dating company Bumble offered all staff a week's break to combat burnout. More recently, Nike announced that it would close its offices worldwide for an additional week over the summer months to "give employees time to recover and rest."[112] On the one hand, these moves acknowledge that burnout is real.[113] On the other hand, it is tokenism in the extreme.

When it comes to the way in which organizations are responding to burnout, some are falling dismally short[114] but others are clearly trying to reimagine a fairer, healthier workplace. For example, there has been a rise in the 'work-from-anywhere' phenomenon,[115] which heralds choice, flexibility, the end of the daily commute and an improved work–life balance for many employees. For example, in 2020 Australia-based software company Atlassian introduced its Team Anywhere policy, offering its 7,000-strong workforce the opportunity to move to any Atlassian site around the world.[116] Two years later and around 10% of the company's staff had relocated. Relocated employees cite advantages such as being closer to family, reduced living costs and gaining a healthier lifestyle,[117] but if the work-from-anywhere phenomenon brings such benefits, why have only one in ten employees taken it up? Atlassian's offer, like other work-from-anywhere initiatives,[118] relies on people having the means and desire to relocate; one-size-fits-all approaches to relocation may not work for everyone, such as those with school-aged children or caring responsibilities for elderly relatives. And, while some workers benefit from more flexibility through work-from-anywhere schemes, organizations also benefit by retaining talent, eliminating real estate costs and improving productivity. As such, although such moves in service of improving working conditions are well intended, ultimately they do little more than prune the branches of burnout rather than tackle it at its roots.

Addressing the root causes of burnout may require wholesale system change, such as challenging the basis upon which we currently measure our 'contribution' at work. It may require us, for example, to move beyond time as the primary measure. As working professionals, many of us have become so anxious about justifying our time to clients, or demonstrating our use and utilization to our employers, we even measure ourselves in terms of monetizable hours. For example, during our research, we came across an organization that required all customer-facing employees to demonstrate their individual productivity, with their productivity being measured in 30-minute units. As is common in many sectors, employees were asked to keep timesheets and when their performance reviews came around, anyone who was able to demonstrate 85% or more productivity over an annual period was awarded a smiley emoticon ☺. Anyone who found themselves between 50% and 85% productive was awarded a neutral emoticon ☻, and those who were less than 50% productive in any given year were given a sad-faced emoticon ☹. The neutral emoticon was taken as a watchlist, and the sad face triggered a performance conversation. With this time-driven indicator of performance, employees had become so focused on proving their worth, it is no coincidence that staff turnover had begun to increase. It has been suggested that organizations should move to outcome-based work as a means of unshackling employees from the time–productivity equation.[119] One of our co-contributors suggested that to move toward a healthier relationship with our work, it is not only how we measure our impact, but also how important we see work in relation to our lives overall:

"Perhaps if we work less, we loosen the grip work has on us in terms of being defined by our work. We need to disentangle ourselves from our identity being wrapped up in what we do and this comes from working less and caring less about work."

There may already be moves afoot in this regard, with over 10,000 employees worldwide trialling a four-day work week as of mid-2022.[120] But, despite widespread enthusiasm for shortening the standard working week, it remains to be seen whether this simply creates pressure on employees in different ways. As one article suggests, the four-day week campaign wrongly assumes that 100% productivity is possible, and its blanket approach fails to take into account individuals' needs and circumstances.[121] Furthermore, given what we know about the gendered nature of burnout, in calling for less work as well as better conditions for work, we also need to ensure that shorter working weeks do not simply replace one form of labour with another, with working parents in particular then replacing their professional roles with domestic chores on 'non-working' days.

During our research for this book, we looked for examples of organizations that are attempting to change the way in which employee contribution is measured. We were hoping to find consciously compassionate companies that value people as much as profit.[122] However, such examples appear to be few and far between. In our search, we came across one US-based consulting company, called NOBL Collective, which appears to be attempting at systemic change. Its mission is to be "the essential partner for ambitious and compassionate leaders everywhere." And its vision is "to improve work and culture for more than a million people before we are ten years old."[123] This company, with its fully remote workforce, appears to be striving to practise what it preaches when it comes to establishing and promoting a healthy culture.[124] In an article about the forming of their culture published on their website it says:

"What if we ... added a more exacting definition of what we hoped and expected for – and from – each other? In addition – what if we spelled out the steps an employee should take if they felt like the organization or its people were no longer respecting the culture they set out to build?"[125]

Through this process, it appears that NOBL's cultural contract was born. Its cultural contract has been reproduced with their permission and is shown in Figure 1

WHAT WE OWE OUR PEOPLE		
Compassion for you as a fellow human being	Even at the cost of ...	Being the fastest, or the most efficient or the most results-oriented organization
A psychologically safe team environment	Even at the cost of ...	A competitive workplace
Time to restore yourself	Even at the cost of ...	Maximum efficiency

WHAT THIS MIGHT LOOK LIKE
(AKA EMBLEMATIC BEHAVIORS)

Starting every meeting with a quick check-in to understand how everyone is doing.

Playing social games with each other during work hours.

Limiting our project allocations to ensure we have time for self-care and to bond internally.

Twice a year, blocking off an entire week for a company retreat.

A monthly team retrospective to improve how we work together.

WHAT WE ASK OF YOU		
Acceptance of others	Even at the cost of ...	Being comfortable
Candor and feedback	Even at the cost of ...	Self-preservation

POSSIBLE EARLY WARNING SIGNS (CALL THESE OUT)
For leaders, a pattern of over-allocating your team and ignoring self-care and internal culture work in favour of immediate client demands.
Only making time for your local team and/or not attending global meetings.
Choosing to work in an unsustainable way.
Letting interpersonal conflicts fester.
Consistently staying quiet during check-ins, or reserving feedback during team retros, project retros, and 1:1s.

WHAT TO DO IF WE BREAK THIS CONTRACT
If you feel like this contract has been seriously violated:
Talk directly to any person or persons involved to determine if a misunderstanding has taken place.
AND/OR report the issue to your location lead or to the Global Board.
If the issue is deemed to not be an unfortunate misunderstanding, the Global Board should open an investigation and transparently share the process and findings with the full company.

FIGURE 1: NOBL'S CULTURAL CONTRACT[126]

If we are to make the changes required to tackle burnout at its roots, we must also demand different working conditions, with employees and employers (like NOBL Collective) seeking to co-create a shared vision of what it means to lead a healthy work life and of how work fits into a life well lived. In NOBL's cultural contract, for example, compassion for self and for others appears to be prioritized, even at the expense of productivity. NOBL appears to be as concerned about its people's collective wellbeing as it is about its profits. The company affirms that purpose also comes from leisure, not just from work. Its cultural vision makes explicit what it hopes and expects for and from its employees, and it aspires to realize these ideas in a community with everyone holding each other to account. Given the scarcity of companies like NOBL, one of our hopes for this research is that enterprises might rethink how they truly make the personal sustainability of their people one of their guiding strengths.

While those employers who are concerned about addressing burnout can take steps to improve the conditions of work, we also have a responsibility as individuals to notice and recognize the disconnect as it emerges between our aspirations for work and our lived experience of work itself. We understood from those who have contributed to our research that some people find themselves so dependent on their work as a means of self-worth that they become unable to detach, despite becoming increasingly dissatisfied with their day-to-day experiences of work. Some of our co-contributors talked about having become so seduced by the material benefits of work, such as salary and status, that they felt unable to get out. Others talked about how the "promise" of reward and the metaphorical pot of gold at the end of the rainbow had kept them striving until the point at which they burnt out and could give no more. It is for these reasons that the answers to burnout not only lie at the doors of employers but also belong to us as individuals. In the move toward eradicating burnout, work should play *a* part, but not *the whole* part, in bringing purpose to our lives, with us deriving meaning from other domains such as our hobbies, volunteering activities, community work, families, friendships and creative endeavours. If we are to truly tackle burnout, this must happen collectively with each of us holding one another to account in ways that honour our dignity and our humanity.

With collective responsibility in mind, we convened two inquiry groups as part of our research for this book. As related in *Chapter 3*, 14 people participated in these groups, which included some people who had experienced burnout in the past, some who were currently in burnout or at least perilously close, and others who felt they were at risk of burning out. Each group convened for 90 minutes each week over six weeks. During one of our group discussions, we asked people to imagine a future without burnout. In this conversation, some people talked of a future where organizational 'health indices' would be deemed as important as organizational 'wealth indices,' with employers held to account when it came to fostering health over profit. Others imagined a future where individual remuneration and reward would become a thing of the past and all remuneration, incentives and rewards would be shared collectively as a means of dampening self-interest and promoting interdependency and shared responsibility. When we asked our co-contributors what their relationship with work would need to look like for them to be able to flourish in a future without burnout, people said the following:

"To feel equal power to my employer in the sense that I'm not a slave to my work."

"The ability to make my own choices."

"Being part of a listening system."

"Feeling truly trusted and valued."

"To not care – it's just a job."

"Finding fulfilment and enjoyment in domains outside of work."

"Being in control of my own contribution."

"Connectedness to my team, my manager and my colleagues."

"Being fairly compensated."

"To not feel imprisoned by corporate benefits."

"To feel that the energy I give to my work is met with equal and reciprocal energy coming back."

"Ultimate freedom and flexibility."

"To feel that my organizational processes don't depersonalize and stifle humanity."

Some of these changes appear to be low-hanging fruit, such as fair compensation, connectedness to colleagues, organizational processes that do not depersonalize, and feeling trusted and valued. For employers who wish to take burnout seriously, these shifts seem entirely possible. In contrast, the shared hopes of ultimate freedom and flexibility, having equal power to one's employer, and being in control of one's own contribution appear to speak to the societal shifts Jonathan Malesic writes of when he suggests that the end of burnout will only come if we collectively reimagine human potential in terms of achieving complete autonomy and self-determination within and outside of work.[127] In our group conversations, people arrived at the same conclusion by reflecting that the answers to burnout lie not only in organizations but also within us. We are ultimately responsible for our own destinies through the choices we make. Other group members talked about responsibility being two-way between individuals and organizations, with line managers in particular having a key role to play. For example, until burnout is destigmatized and we feel able to speak up and talk about our experiences openly at work, we may never fully eliminate burnout.

In an imagined future without burnout, our group co-contributors saw organizations designed around the concept of reciprocity and called for society to radically reimagine the way organizations are structured in order to loosen the routines and processes that stifle and control. Group members imagined future organizations as 'listening' systems in which people treat one another with unconditional positive regard. In these future organizations, co-workers are 'other-focused' as opposed to self-focused, are strongly connected and in tune with one another's needs, and are regularly contracting and re-contracting around the work. In these imagined systems, members are constantly learning, reviewing and rethinking their roles, their culture and their values together in community. The idea of reciprocity became central to an imagined future in our group conversations, with reciprocity being seen as a two-way flow of giving and receiving in organizations. One of the reasons why reciprocity was so important to our co-contributors was because they saw it as the antithesis of their current reality at work. As one of them said:

"Burnout is less about the energy I'm expending and is more about how little I am getting back from colleagues and from the organization."

Someone else talked about how initiatives around a four-day week, unlimited holiday allowance and corporate perks only go so far in 'filling your cup' – with all the energy she gave to her work, her 'cup' soon became empty again. We know from existing research that teams built on principles of reciprocity have increased cohesion, belonging, relational commitment and mutual trust.[128] Furthermore, research suggests that in organizations designed around reciprocity – incorporating practices such as hiring for relational skills, using participatory selection processes, focusing on group incentives and rewards, fostering relational meeting practices and using collaborative technologies – reciprocity becomes a virtuous and generative process, both enhancing the sense of community and improving performance.[129]

When we asked our inquiry group members what they would need to be true about their relationship with work for them to feel balanced, resourced and flourishing, those who were currently in the middle of burnout said they found it difficult to imagine the future. When we met with them, their experience was so immediate and so raw, it was simply about living from day to day. When asked what would help them here and now, unprompted they said "these conversations." It became clear that in these groups of people convened around the common theme of burnout, each of them had found a space to talk in confidence and to start to make sense of what they were going through. "Hope comes from these conversations," someone said. Those who felt at risk of burning out said that our group conversations had helped them to distinguish between the day-to-day stresses and strains of work and the toxicity that they felt was so unhealthy and dangerous. Others said that the group conversations had helped them to become more aware of when they were in overdrive at work and to appreciate that there were other paths or choices they could make (some of the group members decided to hand in their notice and leave their organizations during the period in which our inquiry groups convened). Those people who were looking at their own burnout through the rear-view mirror, having experienced burnout in the past, said that they felt the group conversations were an important reminder of their own fragility and that they had helped them not to fall back into burnout.

It was during these group conversations that we realized there is no panacea for burnout. Each person in the inquiry groups had taken a different path in, and each of them would take a different path out of burnout. This led us to acknowledge that we would not be writing a book that offered people *the* answer. We wrestled with this for some time, having seen the voracious appetite among managers, leaders and HR professionals in the course of our own work for top tips and shortcuts. Interestingly, it was not research findings that brought us answers; rather, it was in the process of convening inquiry groups that we began to see a way ahead. Over the course of the six weeks in which our inquiry groups met, the healing power of conversation and talking with strangers became clear. In the process of bringing together 14 people who were unknown to each other at the start of the research, yet who were all touched by burnout in some way, a deep sense of community began to grow.

Given the strength of support for the inquiry group process, we began to conceive of a social movement that we would call Running on Empty Rounds akin to the Schwartz Center Rounds®.[130] Schwartz Center Rounds enable staff in healthcare organizations (predominantly in Ireland, the United Kingdom and the United States) to talk about the emotional impact of their work. They run monthly and each round is based on a theme, with two or three members of staff talking about their experience and other attending staff having an opportunity to listen, support and build mutual understanding. Schwartz Center Rounds have been found to reduce psychological distress, improve wellbeing and foster teamwork, which ultimately affects the quality of patient care.[131] Given the prevalence of burnout across job roles and industries, one of our hopes from this research is to bring people together who are affected by burnout, to create listening spaces and hosted conversations in Running on Empty Rounds (www.runningonemptyrounds.com). As we draw this research to a close, one thing is certain and that is that we will not eradicate burnout alone. Individuals, organizations and societies will all need to play their part to move us beyond self-interest and toward reciprocity and collective action in order to design future workplaces for the benefit of all.

EPILOGUE:
CLOSING WORDS FROM KATHERINE

The opening decades of the 21st century have been a time of abundance in much of the world. Even in the most challenging environments and underserved communities there is a deluge of information, services and, as the authors of the 2012 book *Abundance* put it, access to possibilities.[132] A Masai villager with a mobile phone has access to more information and services than the president of the United States did just a few decades back. In wealthy communities, this abundance extends to food, education, services and all sorts of consumer goods. There is far more of all this in the Global North than we are able to consume. The abundance that the book by this name advocates for is an aspirational abundance that prioritizes the sustainability of our planet and our species. But if we look at the abundance that already exists today, particularly in developed economies, there is a distortion between what we need or even want and the amount of stuff within our reach. Related to this abundance is the organizational imperative to keep growing our enterprises at an ever-increasing rate. Companies are valued according to their growth potential and their consistent ability to meet that promise.

Jan Eeckhout has written about the astronomical growth of today's mega-companies through their unbridled acquisition of market power.[133] Contrary to the adage that a rising tide lifts all boats, Eeckhout describes what he calls a "profit paradox," in which the economic and market muscle that the Amazons, Googles, Microsofts and others have built for their companies and their top executives is in direct opposition to the value of work itself. If work is devalued, then ordinary workers must work more to maintain the same lifestyle. The price of goods (such as your iPhone) and the valuation of the company (and therefore executive compensation) keep going up, while workers below the very top of the pyramid continue to earn the same wages and are less and less able to buy the goods and services that these companies provide. Eeckhout lays out the economic and social causes and effects of this phenomenon, suggesting that the unchecked size and market power of these firms are destroying the value of work. Given what we have discovered and argued in this book, we see the link where devalued work leads to overwork and burnout, for the sake of maintaining the ever-accelerating growth of the world's leading organizations.

What are the alternatives to more unnecessary abundance and growth? How can we keep ourselves personally safe from feeding a machine that is not going to give many of us a better life? And, organizationally speaking, how can we guard against feeding the health of our people to this machine?

Since the end of 2020, after the strictest COVID-19 lockdowns were eased, I have been living in the countryside an hour north of the big city that had been my home since I was five. My husband was adamant about never being locked down in a city again, our kids had all left to study or work somewhere else, and we were free to make a change. So, while I was apprehensive about leaving the nest that had held us for 20 years and seen our children grow up, I embraced the adventure and came to the Valley of the Horses.[134] The change has been radical, sometimes challenging, but mostly highly energizing and rewarding. Working online, featuring long days on video calls, I turned to gardening as a source of solace, reconnection with myself and a means of getting to know the land that was slowly becoming my home. A patchwork of rich volcanic soil is interspersed with hard, crumbly Mediterranean crust. What grows here is a whole journey of discovery and adaptation. I am amazed by the lessons in gardens: when you give something energy and attention, it tends to grow; sometimes you do these things and it dies anyway; overwatering and stagnant water rot the roots; juicy fruit happens slowly; pruning unnecessary branches makes the other branches thrive; worms are good; dogs can be dangerous.

From the perspective of our embodied mental and physical health, in which a balance of everything is the key to sustainability, abundance, excessive growth and the mega-company mentality are the primary threats that risk throwing off not only our personal sustainability and wellbeing, but also that of the planet. In this book we have looked at a variety of practices and approaches that can keep us connected to our sources of energy and health. In a world in which several billion of us were able to consciously engage in these practices and remain aware of ourselves and of others around us, there could emerge a movement that was more conscious, more connected, less seduced by growth and more nurturing of people and planet. When I had four small children and a full-time job, many people would ask me how I did it. My answer was this: it is different every day and every day I have to adjust. Ironically, I never felt close to burnout until my kids were grown and out of the house. Perhaps I lost the perspective that being a parent of young children afforded me and therefore threw myself unchecked into a vortex of work. Or perhaps the demands on me (by my work and myself) became greater.

Whatever the causes, we have discovered through our own experiences and in our research for this book that the first and most important step in staying whole is noticing what is happening to us. The next is engaging in practices that hold us back from the flames of burnout and keep us noticing evermore. The heartening part of this simple realization about noticing is that while we cannot change others' habits, we can notice them for ourselves and for each other. In closing, it is our hope that this book and the Running on Empty Rounds become a *space and time for noticing* that we hold for ourselves and for each other in order to treasure the space and time we have on Earth.

POSTSCRIPT

This book documents a moment in time, both personally and historically, for the people who have taken part in this research. But life inevitably moves forward and so we wanted to capture how some of our contributors are now, some months on, as a reminder that burnout does not go away or get eradicated or extracted from us. Those affected, despite having moved forward, continue to live in its shadow. Because more than the phenomenon of people overworking and organizations capitalizing on our overwork, it is the lived experience of burnout that we have tried to portray here. As can be expected in the human experience, there are a variety of ways in which our co-contributors have moved forward. Some have re-prioritized the role work plays in their lives; others have fallen into burnout again; and others have had knock-on health afflictions. This is also the case for us, as authors. As a result of what we have learned over the two years we have spent researching for this book, about ourselves and our own relationship with overwhelm and burnout, we have each made changes to our lives. I (Amy) took the decision to step back from full-time employment and, in parallel, we decided to make a move to southwest France. My husband and I have found a little corner of the Pyrenees that has a deep calling for me in particular. We live there in stripped back simplicity and are held by the mountains that surround us. This place feels a million miles away from the pace, pressure and demands of work life and is our place to just be.

In all the co-contributors to this research, the experience of participation and particularly the reliving of their experiences through reading our accounts of their stories has had a profound impact, suggesting to us that remaining in open dialogue about burnout is helpful whether we are in the process of healing, navigating its dangers, or finding ways to keep it at bay. In their own words, the testimonials below speak to the effects that we hope our Running on Empty Rounds (www.runningonemptyrounds. com) will have moving forward, that is to say where we host confidential conversations among strangers about their experiences of burnout and the practices that can help us prevent and heal:

"Professionally and personally, I have to admit it was quite emotional to read this. At Christmas I was hospitalized with a suspected stroke. In the end everything was fine and there is no lasting damage but reading your words I realized that those were the same words I used when I was in hospital - shutting down - the comment about the MacBook. I guess I was naive to think that I could dance on the edge." (Igor)

"It's fascinating to read it back now I'm 'out of the other side'; it is simultaneously painful and rewarding to think of what I lived through." (Brian)

"It was rewarding to participate in the community research component. I learned a lot through your reflective process with us and also from the others in the community. It was insightful and really helpful in my own recovery journey." (Britta)

"I'm just about to celebrate my 51st birthday. As I reflect on the last year, I feel both a sense of relief and disbelief. It's been a bitch of a year. And ironically I'd wanted it to be my best. This very same time one year ago, the night before my 50th birthday, my reflection was how hard I'd worked on myself in the year leading up to turning 50, so that I would step into and over that mark as the person I wanted to be. But what happened is that I stepped over and fell off. I had all the tools and the knowledge, but it still happened to me and what I now know, just like with depression, is that it is always there lurking. You need to be aware, treat yourself kindly and compassionately and most importantly have the strength to know your boundaries and set them … at home, at work, with yourself … so that you don't fall prey to burnout, depression, addiction, or whatever your go to is when it all gets too hard." (Ananya)

In closing, we urge you, our readers, to open a process of dialogue in your families, communities, teams and organizations, as it is clear that overwhelm and burnout present an ongoing and profound challenge.

We must keep burnout in view and as part of an ongoing conversation about organizational life – just as we might talk about business threats such as price wars, climate change or potential economic recessions – if we are to flourish as people and as co-contributors to the organizations that shape our present and future societies.

ACKNOWLEDGEMENTS

Without our co-contributors, this book would not have been possible. We would like to thank each of them for their courage and generosity, and for trusting us.

Alaina, Antoinette, Chelsea, Dan, Elaine, Georgie, Ian, James, Matt, Malcolm, Pierre, Salima, Sally, Simon and Steve

Last but not least, a loving thanks to each of our partners, Col and Sam, for their support, patience and dedication to navigating life with us. They are an irreplaceable source of sustenance in our work and in our lives.

ENDNOTES

1. Bartleby, "Remote workers work longer not more efficiently," *The Economist*, 10 June 2021, https://www.economist.com/business/2021/06/10/remote-workers-work-longer-not-more-efficiently.

2. Abramson, A., "Burnout and stress are everywhere," *American Psychological Association*, 1 January 2022, https://www.apa.org/monitor/2022/01/special-burnout-stress.

3. Moss, J., *The Burnout Epidemic: The Rise of Chronic Stress and How We Can Fix It* (Harvard Business Review Press, 2021).

4. Ducharme, J., "The 'Great Resignation' is finally getting companies to take burnout seriously – is it enough?," *Time*, 14 October 2021, https://time.com/6106656/workplace-burnout-pandemic.

5. Wright Mills, C., *Power, Politics, and People: The Collected Essays of C. Wright Mills* (Oxford University Press, 1963).

6. Freudenberger, H. J., "Staff burn-out," *Journal of Social Issues*, Vol. 30, No. 1 (1974), pp. 159–165.

7. Maslach C., *Burnout: The Cost of Caring* (Prentice-Hall, 1974).

8. Lepore, J., "Burnout: Modern affliction or human condition?" *New Yorker*, 24 May 2021, https://www.newyorker.com/magazine/2021/05/24/burnout-modern-affliction-or-human-condition.

9. Ghandi, V. & Robison, J. "The 'Great Resignation' is really the 'Great Discontent'," *Gallup*, 22 July 2021, https://www.gallup.com/workplace/351545/great-resignation-really-great-discontent.aspx.

10. Ibid.

11. Leiter, M. P. & Maslach, C., "Latent burnout profiles: A new approach to understanding the burnout experience," *Burnout Research*, Vol. 3, No. 4 (2016), pp. 89–100.

12. Maté, G., *In the Realm of Hungry Ghosts: Close Encounters with Addiction* (Penguin Random House, 2018), p. xvii.

13. Grant, A., "That lockdown blah you're feeling? It's called languishing. Here's how to beat it," *Irish Times*, 22 April 2021, https://www.irishtimes.com/life-and-style/health-family/that-lockdown-blah-you-re-feeling-it-s-called-languishing-here-s-how-to-beat-it-1.4542469.

14. *ILO Monitor: COVID-19 and the World of Work – Seventh Edition*, International Labour Organization, 2021, https://www.ilo.org/wcmsp5/groups/public/---dgreports/---dcomm/documents/briefingnote/wcms_767028.pdf.

15. Kramer, S., "With billions confined to their homes worldwide, which living arrangements are most common?" *Pew Research Center*, 31 March 2020, https://www.pewresearch.org/fact-tank/2020/03/31/with-billions-confined-to-their-homes-worldwide-which-living-arrangements-are-most-common.

16. Forbes, D. L., "Toward a unified model of human motivation," *Review of General Psychology*, Vol. 15, No. 2 (2011), pp. 85–98.

17. Levine, S. & Ursin, H., "What is stress?" in Brown, M. R., Koob, G. F. & Rivier, C. (eds), *Stress, Neurobiology and Neuroendocrinology* (Marcel Dekker, 1991), pp. 3–21.

18. *ILO Monitor*. Op. cit.

19. Schmall, T., "Almost half of Americans consider themselves 'workaholics'," *New York Post*, 1 February 2019, https://nypost.com/2019/02/01/almost-half-of-americans-consider-themselves-workaholics.

20. Asberg, M., quoted in Moss, *The Burnout Epidemic*, Op. cit., p 7.

21. Maslach, C., "Burn-out," *Human Behavior*, Vol. 5 (1976), pp. 16–22.

22. Freudenberger, H. J., Op. cit.

23. Maslach, C., Schaufeli, W. B. & Leiter, M. P., "Job burnout," *Annual Review of Psychology*, Vol. 52, No. 1 (2001), pp. 397–422.

24. Morgan, K., "Why we may be measuring burnout all wrong," *BBC Worklife*, 29 April 2021, https://www.bbc.com/worklife/article/20210426-why-we-may-be-measuring-burnout-all-wrong.

25. Leiter & Maslach, Latent burnout profiles, Op. cit.

26. Maslach, C. & Leiter, M. P., "Reversing burnout," *Stanford Social Innovation Review*, Winter (2005), pp. 43–49.

27. Ibid., p. 49.

28. Maslach, C. & Leiter, M. P., "Early predictors of job burnout and engagement," *Journal of Applied Psychology*, Vol. 93, No. 3 (2008), p. 498.

29. Leiter, M. P., Hakanen, J. J., Ahola, K., Toppinen-Tanner, S., Koskinen, A. & Väänänen, A., "Organizational predictors and health consequences of changes in burnout: A 12-year cohort study," *Journal of Organizational Behavior*, Vol. 34, No. 7 (2013), pp. 959–973.

30. Day, A. & Leiter, M. P., "The good and bad of working relationships: Implications for burnout," in Leiter, M. P., Bakker, A. B. & Maslach, C. (eds), *Burnout at Work: A Psychological Perspective* (Psychology Press, 2014), pp. 56–79.

31. Breevaart, K., Bakker, A. B., Hetland, J. & Hetland, H., "The influence of constructive and destructive leadership behaviors on follower burnout," in Leiter, M. P., Bakker, A. B. & Maslach, C. (eds), *Burnout at Work: A Psychological Perspective* (Psychology Press, 2014), pp. 102–121.

32. Maslach, C. & Jackson S. E., "The measurement of experienced burnout," *Organizational Behavior*, Vol. 2, No. 2 (1981), pp. 99–113.

33. Calhoun, L. G. & Tedeschi, R. G. (eds), *Handbook of Posttraumatic Growth: Research and Practice* (Lawrence Erlbaum Associates, 2006).

34. Bianchi, R., Schonfeld, I. S. & Laurent, E., "Burnout: Moving beyond the status quo," *International Journal of Stress Management*, Vol. 26, No. 1 (2019), p. 36.

35. Leiter, M. P., Bakker, A. B. & Maslach, C., *Burnout at Work: A Psychological Perspective* (Psychology Press, 2014), p. 3.

36. Jaffe, S., *Work Won't Love You Back: How Devotion to Our Jobs Keeps Us Exploited, Exhausted and Alone* (Hurst and Company, 2021).

37. Malesic, J., *The End of Burnout: Why Work Drains Us and How to Build Better Lives* (University of California Press, 2022), p. 2.

38. Ibid.

39. Kothari, A., "Battling burnout: A conversation with resiliency expert Dr. Amit Sood," *McKinsey & Company*, 7 December 2021, https://www.mckinsey.com/industries/healthcare-systems-and-services/our-insights/battling-burnout-a-conversation-with-resiliency-expert-dr-amit-sood.

40. Hempel, J., "Beating burnout with Emily and Amelia Nagoski," *Hello Monday*, 8 November 2021, https://podcasts.apple.com/us/podcast/hello-monday-with-jessi-hempel/id1453893304?i=1000500764886.

41. Morgan, K., "Can 'sleep leadership' help banish burnout?" *BBC Worklife*, 18 January 2022, https://www.bbc.com/worklife/article/20220114-can-sleep-leadership-help-banish-burnout.

42. *Employee Burnout: Causes and Cures*, Gallup, 2022, https://www.gallup.com/workplace/282659/employee-burnout-perspective-paper.aspx.

43. Wengraf, T., "Preparing lightly-structured depth interviews: A design for a BNIM-type biographic-narrative interview," in *Qualitative Research Interviewing: Biographic Narrative and Semi-Structured Methods* (Sage, 2001), pp. 111–151.

44. Neimeyer, R., "Re-storying loss: Fostering growth in the posttraumatic narrative," in Calhoun, L. G. & Tedeschi, R. G. (eds), *Handbook of Posttraumatic Growth: Research and Practice* (Lawrence Erlbaum Associates, 2006), pp. 68–81.

45. Neiderhoffer, K. G. & Pennebaker, J. W., "Sharing one's story: On the benefits of writing or talking about emotional experience," in Lopez, S. J. & Snyder, C. R. (eds), *Oxford Handbook of Positive Psychology* (Oxford University Press, 2009), pp. 621–633.

46. Harari, Y. N., *Homo Deus: A Brief History of Tomorrow* (Random House, 2016).

47. Ibid, p. 149.

48. Ibid, p. 151.

49. Eeckhout, J., *The Profit Paradox: How Thriving Firms Threaten the Future of Work* (Princeton University Press, 2021).

50. Peterson, U., Demerouti, E., Bergström, G., Samuelsson, M., Asberg, M. & Nygren, A., "Burnout and physical and mental health among Swedish healthcare workers," *Journal of Advanced Nursing*, Vol. 62, No. 1 (2008), pp. 84–95.

51. Dalton-Smith, S., *Sacred Rest: Recover Your Life, Renew Your Energy, Restore Your Sanity* (Hachette, 2017).

52. Gilbert, P., *The Compassionate Mind* (Constable, 2010).

53. Neff, K. & Germer, G., *The Mindful Self-Compassion Workbook* (Guildford Press, 2018).

54. Janoff-Bulman, R., "Schema-change perspectives on posttraumatic growth," in Calhoun, L. G. & Tedeschi, R. G. (eds), *Handbook of Posttraumatic Growth: Research & Practice* (Lawrence Erlbaum Associates, 2006), p. 86.

55. Post-traumatic stress disorder (PTSD), *Mind*, 2022, https://www.mind.org.uk/information-support/types-of-mental-health-problems/post-traumatic-stress-disorder-ptsd-and-complex-ptsd/symptoms.

56. Khazan, O., "Only your boss can cure your burnout," *The Atlantic*, 12 March 2021, https://www.theatlantic.com/politics/archive/2021/03/how-tell-if-you-have-burnout/618250.

57. Neiderhoffer & Pennebaker, Op. cit.

58. Neimeyer, Op. cit.

59. Kohler Riessman, C., *Narrative Methods for the Human Sciences* (Sage, 2008).

60. Leiter, M. P., Bakker, A. B. & Maslach, C., "The contemporary contex of job burnout," in Leiter, M. P., Bakker, A. B. & Maslach, C. (eds), *Burnout at Work: A Psychological Perspective* (Psychology Press, 2014), pp. 1–9.

61. Maslach & Leiter, Op. cit.

62. Steffens, N. K., Haslam, S. A., Jetten, J. & van Dick, R., "A meta-analytic review of social identification and health in organizational contexts," *Personality and Social Psychology Review*, Vol. 21, No. 4 (2017), pp. 305–335.

63. Avanzi, L., Savadori, L., Fraccaroli, F., Ciampa, V. & van Dick, R., "Too-much-of-a-good-thing? The curvilinear relation between identification, overcommitment, and employee wellbeing," *Current Psychology*, Vol. 41 (2022), p. 1259.

64. Ibid.

65. Conroy, S., Henle, C. A., Shore, L. & Stelman, S., "Where there is light, there is dark: A review of the detrimental outcomes of high organizational identification," *Journal of Organizational Behavior*, Vol. 38, No. 2 (2017), pp. 184–203.

66. Siegrist, J., "Effort–reward imbalance and health in a globalized economy," *Scandinavian Journal of Work, Environment & Health Supplement*, Vol. 6 (2008), p. 164.

67. Stoeber, J. & Damian, L. E., "Perfectionism in employees: Work engagement, workaholism, and burnout," in Sirois, F. M. & Molnar, D. S. (eds), *Perfectionism, Health, and Wellbeing* (Springer, 2016), pp. 265–283.

68. Ibid.

69. Ibid.

70. Ibid

71. Stress effects on the body, *American Psychological Association*, 1 November 2018, https://www.apa.org/topics/stress/body.

72. Seladi-Schulman, J., "How stress increases your risk of heart disease," *Healthline*, 7 February 2022, https://www.healthline.com/health/heart-disease/stress-is-a-factor-that-contributes-to-heart-disease-risk.

73. Deligkaris, P., Panagopoulou, E., Montgomery, A. J. & Masoura, E., "Job burnout and cognitive functioning: A systematic review," *Work & Stress*, Vol. 28, No. 2 (2014), pp. 107–123.

74. Laderer, A., Why do I feel numb? *Talkspace*, 10 July 2020, https://www.talkspace.com/blog/numb-numbness-causes-solutions-why-do-i-feel.

75. Patrichi, B. E., Ene, C., Rîndașu, C., & Trifu, A. C. (2021). Dissociative Amnesia and Dissociative Identity Disorder. *Journal of Educational Sciences & Psychology*, Vol 11, No 1, pp 207-216.

76. Schaufeli, W. B., Leiter, M. P. & Maslach, C., "Burnout: 35 years of research and practice," *Career Development International*, Vol. 14 (2009), pp. 204–220.

77. *State of the Global Workplace: 2022 Report,* https://www.gallup.com/workplace/349484/state-of-the-global-workplace.aspx.

78. Breevaart et al., Op. cit.

79. Tepper, B. J., "Consequences of abusive supervision," *Academy of Management Journal*, Vol. 43, No. 2 (2000), pp. 178–190.

80. Veldsman, T., "How toxic leaders destroy people as well as organizations," *The Conversation*, 14 January 2016, https://theconversation.com/how-toxic-leaders-destroy-people-as-well-as-organizations-51951.

81. Breevaart et al., Op. cit.

82. Skogstad, A., Einarsen, S. V., Torsheim, T., Aasland, M. S. & Hetland, H., "The destructiveness of laissez-faire leadership behavior," *Journal of Occupational Health Psychology*, Vol. 12, No. 1, pp. 80–92.

83. Veldsman, Op. cit.

84. "Everything you need to know about pushing for equal pay," *UN Women*, 14 September 2020, https://www.unwomen.org/en/news/stories/2020/9/explainer-everything-you-need-to-know-about-equal-pay.

85. Foley, M., Oxenbridge, S., Cooper, R. & Baird, M. "'I'll never be one of the boys': Gender harassment of women working as pilots and automotive tradespeople," *Gender, Work & Organization*, 9 March 2020, https://doi.org/10.1111/gwao.12443.

86. Lungumbu, S. & Butterly, A. "Coronavirus and gender: More chores for women set back gains in equality," *BBC News*, 26 November 2020, https://www.bbc.co.uk/news/world-55016842.

87. Aldossari, M. & Chaudhry, S., "Women and burnout in the context of a pandemic," *Gender, Work & Organization*, Vol. 28, No. 2, pp. 826–834.

88. Rosa Royle, O., "Why offering staff a week off work won't fix burnout," *Management Today*, 27 April 2021, https://www.managementtoday.co.uk/why-offering-staff-week-off-work-wont-fix-burnout/food-for-thought/article/1713366.

89. Treglown, L., Palaiou, K., Zarola, A. & Furnham, A., "The dark side of resilience and burnout: A moderation-mediation model," *PloS One*, Vol. 11, No. 6 (2016), e0156279.

90. Svoboda, E., "Tough compassion: Here's what it is and why you need to practice it," Ideas.TED.com, 22 June 2021, https://ideas.ted.com/tough-compassion-heres-what-it-is-and-why-you-need-to-practice-it.

91. Ibid.

92. van der Kolk, B., *The Body Keeps the Score: Mind, Brain and Body in the Transformation of Trauma* (Penguin Random House, 2014), p. 282.

93. Ibid, p. 104.

94. Walsh, M., *Embodiment: Moving Beyond Mindfulness*, (Unicorn Slayer Press, 2020).

95. Neff, K. & Germer, C., Op. cit.

96. Bodian, S., *Beyond Mindfulness: The Direct Approach to Lasting Peace, Happiness and Love* (Non-Duality Press, 2017).

97. Young, S., *The Science of Enlightenment: How Meditation Works* (Sounds True, 2016).

98. MacGregor, S. P. & Semler, K., "Towards whole person learning through sustainable executive performance," *Journal of Management Development*, Vol. 31, No. 3 (2012), pp. 231–242.

99. "5 positive effects music has on your mental health," *Open Minds*, 10 February 2020, https://openminds.org.au/news/5-positive-effects-music-mental-health.

100. Begum, T., "How listening to birdsong can transform our mental health," *Natural History Museum*, 8 October 2020, https://www.nhm.ac.uk/discover/how-listening-to-birdsong-can-transform-our-mental-health.html.

101. Marshall, S., "Restore," *Finding Ourselves*, 2021, https://www.drstevemarshall.com/journal/2021/6/24/restore?rq=restore.

102. Bolton, G., "'Every poem breaks a silence that had to be overcome': The therapeutic power of poetry writing," *Feminist Review*, Vol. 62, No. 1 (1999), pp. 118–133.

103. van der Kolk, Op. cit.

104. Scharmer, O. & Kaufer, K., *Leading from the Emerging Future* (Berrett-Koehler, 2013).

105. Capra, F., *The Web of Life: A New Scientific Understanding of Living Systems* (Anchor Books, 1997).

106. van der Kolk, Op. cit., p229.

107. Ibid.

108. Hochschild, A.R. (1979). Emotion work, feeling rules, and social structure. American Journal of Sociology, 85(3), 551-575.

109. Ibid, p. 228.

110. Dweck, C., *Mindset: The New Psychology of Success* (Penguin Random House, 2006).

111. *State of the Global Workplace Report*, Op. cit.

112. Ciment, S., "Here's how Nike, Lululemon, Nordstrom + more are balancing mental health priorities with return-to-office," *Footwear News*, 9 May 2022, https://footwearnews-com.cdn.ampproject. org/c/s/footwearnews.com/2022/business/retail/ retailers-balance-mental-health-during-return-to- office-1203284099/amp.

113. Jones, L., "Bumble closes to give 'burnt-out' staff a week's break," *BBC News*, 21 June 2021, https://www- bbc-com.cdn.ampproject.org/c/s/www.bbc.com/news/ business-57562230.amp.

114. Louis, S., "Worker beware: These are the 22 worst companies to work for," *MoneyWise*, 10 December 2020, https://moneywise.com/employment/the-worst- companies-to-work-for.

115. Choudhury, P., "Our work-from-anywhere future," *Harvard Business Review*, November–December 2020, https://hbr.org/2020/11/our-work-from-anywhere-future.

116. Our distributed workforce, *Atlassian*, 2022, https://www.atlassian.com/practices/use-cases/team-anywhere.

117. Liu, J., "4 people on how their company's switch to work-from-anywhere spurred them to move around the world," *CNBC*, 17 April 2022, https://www.cnbc.com/2022/04/17/4-atlassian-workers-share-how-work-from-anywhere-spurred-them-to-move.html.

118. Begley Bloom, L., "Work from home or anywhere: Top 30 companies for remote jobs in 2022," *Forbes*, 31 January 2022, https://www.forbes.com/sites/laurabegleybloom/2022/01/31/work-from-home-or-anywhere-top-30-companies-for-remote-jobs-in-2022/?sh=4789435b7963.

119. Harper, B., "Hybrid work and outcome-based performance management," *Medium*, 19 August 2021, https://medium.com/slalom-business/hybrid-work-and-outcome-based-performance-management-970db7886c29#:~:text=Outcomes%2Dbased%20performance%20management%20supports,collaborate%20will%20continue%20to%20grow.

120. See https://www.4dayweek.com.

121. Hamilton, C., "The problems with a four-day week," *Unleash*, 4 February 2022, https://www.unleash.ai/future-of-work/the-problems-with-a-four-day-week.

122. Bradley, A., *The Human Moment: The Positive Power of Compassion in the Workplace* (LID Publishing, 2019).

123. "How to hold teams together & accountable with a cultural contract," *NOBL Academy*, 4 February 2020, https://academy.nobl.io/make-shared-ways-of-working-explicit-with-a-cultural-contract.

124. https://nobl.io/

125. Ibid.

126. Cultural Contract (public), *NOBL*, https://docs.google.com/document/d/1WEcjPeNK-HuLkA4Mzsag8Dkr2WCBQHW DeznSTKlFyBU/edit.

127. Malesic, Op. cit., p. 162.

128. Molm, L. D., Collett, J. L. & Schaefer, D. R., "Building solidarity through generalized exchange: A theory of reciprocity," *American Journal of Sociology*, Vol. 113, No. 1 (2007), pp. 205–242.

129. Baker, W., "A dual model of reciprocity in organizations: Moral sentiments and reputation," in Cameron, K. S. & Spreitzer, G. M. (eds), *Oxford Handbook of Positive Organizational Scholarship* (Oxford University Press, 2012), pp. 412–422.

130. See https://www.theschwartzcenter.org.

131. Maben, J., Taylor, C., Dawson, J., Leamy, M., McCarthy, I. & Reynolds, E., "A realist informed mixed methods evaluation of Schwartz Center Rounds® in England," *National Institute for Health and Care Research*, Vol. 6, No. 37 (2018), https://www.journalslibrary.nihr.ac.uk/hsdr/hsdr06370/#/abstract%20.

132. Diamandis, E. & Kotler, S., *Abundance* (Free Press, 2012).

133. Eeckhout, Op. cit.

134. Thanks to Teresa Goode for the unofficial name of our valley and for being one of the treasures we found there.

ABOUT
DR AMY
BRADLEY

DR AMY BRADLEY is a Professor of Leadership and Management and author of *The Human Moment*. In 2020, she was named on the prestigious Thinkers50 Radar of global management thinkers. She contributes as adjunct faculty at several leading business schools and runs her own business, which help leaders and organizations to become more compassionate in an age where our work is increasingly dehumanized. She and her husband Colin live in the UK and have four children between them.

ABOUT DR KATHERINE SEMLER

DR KATHERINE SEMLER partners with leaders and organizations to help them define and live their purpose. She is a partner at Korn Ferry and adjunct faculty at Ashridge Hult International Business School. She lives in Girona, Spain, where she and her husband host group retreats and vacations in a refurbished Catalan farmhouse. They have four children who spend vacations with them in Spain and Maine, USA.